CONTROVERSIES

Factory Farming

WITHDRAWN
PRINT

Other Books in the Current Controversies Series

Factory Farming

Debra A. Miller, Book Editor

GREENHAVEN PRESS
A part of Gale, Cengage Learning

GALE
CENGAGE Learning

Detroit • New York • San Francisco • New Haven, Conn • Waterville, Maine • London

Christine Nasso, *Publisher*
Elizabeth Des Chenes, *Managing Editor*

For more information, contact:
Greenhaven Press
27500 Drake Rd.
Farmington Hills, MI 48331-3535
Or you can visit our Internet site at gale.cengage.com

For product information and technology assistance, contact us at

Gale Customer Support, 1-800-877-4253
For permission to use material from this text or product, submit all requests online at www.cengage.com/permissions

Further permissions questions can be emailed to permissionrequest@cengage.com

Articles in Greenhaven Press anthologies are often edited for length to meet page requirements. In addition, original titles of these works are changed to clearly present the main thesis and to explicitly indicate the author's opinion. Every effort is made to ensure that Greenhaven Press accurately reflects the original intent of the authors. Every effort has been made to trace the owners of copyrighted material.

Cover image copyright © Peter Walton/Monsoon/Photolibrary/Corbis.

LIBRARY OF CONGRESS CATALOGING-IN-PUBLICATION DATA

Factory farming / Debra A. Miller, book editor.
    p. cm. -- (Current controversies)
  Includes bibliographical references and index.
  ISBN 978-0-7377-4909-0 (hardcover) -- ISBN 978-0-7377-4910-6 (pbk.)
  1. Factory farms. 2. Livestock farms. I. Miller, Debra A. II. Series: Current controversies.
  SF140.L58F33 2010
  179'.3--dc22
                                                          2009053380

Printed in the United States of America
1 2 3 4 5 6 7 14 13 12 11 10

Contents

Modern farming techniques used by professional food producers, often criticized as factory farming, have almost completely eradicated the famines that humans have endured throughout history. It is suicidal to abandon these scientific agricultural advances at a time when the Earth's population is growing rapidly.

Today's food animal production systems are much more sophisticated and produce a much higher quality food product than older, "free-range" systems in which animals were exposed to weather, dirty conditions, predators, and disease. Changing those production methods will mean lower production, more disease, lower quality products, and higher food costs.

Many dairy farmers are very passionate about their jobs and do their best to apply best practices and technology to provide a good quality of life for their animals and their employees, as well as protect the environment. They find their work rewarding because they are providing a high-quality product that helps feed the world.

Each part of the livestock and poultry industries has its own educational programs, guidelines, and best-management practices to ensure the highest quality care for animals raised for food. Overzealous standards and regulation will only increase the costs of production and the price of food for consumers.

Almost ten billion farm animals are killed for food each year in the United States. Before they are slaughtered, they endure lives of abuse with virtually no legal protection.

Chapter 3: Does Factory Farming Harm Human Health or the Environment?

Humans' desire for cheap meat has led to mass production of chickens, pigs, and other animals by raising them quickly in crowded, stressful conditions. These conditions serve as incubators for new diseases, such as swine or avian flu, and are the price that society will pay for abusing animals and nature.

Foreword

By definition, controversies are "discussions of questions in which opposing opinions clash" (*Webster's Twentieth Century Dictionary Unabridged*). Few would deny that controversies are a pervasive part of the human condition and exist on virtually every level of human enterprise. Controversies transpire between individuals and among groups, within nations and between nations. Controversies supply the grist necessary for progress by providing challenges and challengers to the status quo. They also create atmospheres where strife and warfare can flourish. A world without controversies would be a peaceful world; but it also would be, by and large, static and prosaic.

The Series' Purpose

The purpose of the *Current Controversies* series is to explore many of the social, political, and economic controversies dominating the national and international scenes today. Titles selected for inclusion in the series are highly focused and specific. For example, from the larger category of criminal justice, *Current Controversies* deals with specific topics such as police brutality, gun control, white collar crime, and others. The debates in *Current Controversies* also are presented in a useful, timeless fashion. Articles and book excerpts included in each title are selected if they contribute valuable, long-range ideas to the overall debate. And wherever possible, current information is enhanced with historical documents and other relevant materials. Thus, while individual titles are current in focus, every effort is made to ensure that they will not become quickly outdated. Books in the *Current Controversies* series will remain important resources for librarians, teachers, and students for many years.

In addition to keeping the titles focused and specific, great care is taken in the editorial format of each book in the series. Book introductions and chapter prefaces are offered to provide background material for readers. Chapters are organized around several key questions that are answered with diverse opinions representing all points on the political spectrum. Materials in each chapter include opinions in which authors clearly disagree as well as alternative opinions in which authors may agree on a broader issue but disagree on the possible solutions. In this way, the content of each volume in *Current Controversies* mirrors the mosaic of opinions encountered in society. Readers will quickly realize that there are many viable answers to these complex issues. By questioning each author's conclusions, students and casual readers can begin to develop the critical thinking skills so important to evaluating opinionated material.

Current Controversies is also ideal for controlled research. Each anthology in the series is composed of primary sources taken from a wide gamut of informational categories including periodicals, newspapers, books, U.S. and foreign government documents, and the publications of private and public organizations. Readers will find factual support for reports, debates, and research papers covering all areas of important issues. In addition, an annotated table of contents, an index, a book and periodical bibliography, and a list of organizations to contact are included in each book to expedite further research.

Perhaps more than ever before in history, people are confronted with diverse and contradictory information. During the Persian Gulf War, for example, the public was not only treated to minute-to-minute coverage of the war, it was also inundated with critiques of the coverage and countless analyses of the factors motivating U.S. involvement. Being able to sort through the plethora of opinions accompanying today's major issues, and to draw one's own conclusions, can be a complicated and frustrating struggle. It is the editors' hope that *Current Controversies* will help readers with this struggle.

Introduction

"Most meats, produce, and other foods found in supermarkets in the United States and abroad come from large, corporate-owned industrial operations, often called factory farms."

Most people think of a farm as a small, family-owned operation where cows graze in open pastures, chickens peck around the yard, and fields are lush with a variety of crops. The reality of modern farming, however, is quite different. Most meats, produce, and other foods found in supermarkets in the United States and abroad come from large, corporate-owned industrial operations, often called factory farms. In fact, according to the research group Worldwatch Institute, 74 percent of the world's poultry, 68 percent of eggs, 50 percent of pork, and 43 percent of beef are now produced by factory farms.

Modern agribusiness farms typically cover thousands of acres, as compared with family-run farms of yesterday, which often were no more than a couple hundred acres. Instead of growing a diverse mix of vegetables, fruits, and grain crops, today's farms focus mostly on a few commodity crops, such as corn, soybeans, and wheat—crops used in many processed foods, exported to other countries, or converted into feed for animals. This is assembly-line farming, where high-tech machinery is used to minimize human labor as much as possible and petroleum-based chemicals, or petro-chemicals, are routinely applied to crops as fertilizers and pesticides.

Similarly, modern livestock, dairy, and chicken/egg producers also are highly specialized factory farms—often called industrial farm animal production (IFAP) or confined animal feeding operations (CAFOs). Animal factory farms house thousands of animals from just a few species in often crowded conditions in huge buildings. The animals are given antibiotics to prevent disease and they are fed special foods and supplements to make them grow or produce quickly. Although there are some laws and guidelines governing how animals should be housed or slaughtered, animals in factory farms are generally treated as production units rather than as living creatures with the right to humane treatment. Critics claim that many standard agribusiness practices cause these farm animals to live lives of constant pain, suffering, and abuse. In fact, in articles and media outlets, the term "factory farm" often is used negatively to refer exclusively to large-scale, industrial animal production facilities.

Although humans have been farming for more than 10,000 years, farming on this large, factory scale is a fairly recent phenomenon—the product of the Industrial Revolution, the discovery of carbon-based fuels, and the development of petroleum-based chemicals. Farming first began to change from labor-intensive, subsistence methods to a much more industrialized operation in the 1800s, when a variety of farm machines were invented to plant, harvest, and process crops. Soon, transportation and food preservation technologies, such as refrigerated railway cars, helped to transport crops to markets.

Following World War II, farming took another major step toward today's farming model when chemical manufacturers, which were previously involved in the war effort, turned their attention to producing pesticides, herbicides, and synthetic fertilizers for American farmers. These petro-chemical products, together with advances in genetic selection and irrigation techniques, helped to produce what became known as the Green Revolution—a worldwide transformation in agriculture that brought dramatic increases in agricultural productivity. During the past half-century, U.S. farmers who could implement these new techniques saw their crop production numbers double or triple. Small farmers, however, often were driven from their farms because they could not compete with the new, larger, more productive factory farms. The new abundance of cheap grains, in turn, made larger-scale animal agriculture operations possible and allowed more Americans to buy meat more often. This American model of farming also was adopted by other developed countries, and many commentators have argued that the productivity gains of the Green Revolution have been instrumental in feeding the Earth's rapidly growing population.

Throughout this period, U.S. farm policies encouraged the development of ever-larger factory farms. The most direct type of government support came in the form of farm subsidies, taxpayer money paid to farmers who grow any of about two dozen commodity crops, such as wheat, cotton, rice, and peanuts. The subsidies work by fixing prices of agricultural goods at levels higher than the market rate. Farm subsidies began during the Great Depression of the 1930s, when economic conditions dramatically lowered the prices of agricultural goods and caused a farm crisis. Once these subsidies were in place, however, farmers viewed them as an entitlement, pressuring Congress to continue them—even expand them—to the present day. In 2007, for example, taxpayers paid approximately $5 billion in direct payment crop subsidies, the bulk of which went to the country's largest, corporate-owned industrial farms.

Today, however, the factory farming system is being challenged as never before. Critics argue that in addition to the abusive treatment of animals and the death of family-owned farms, the system is simply environmentally unsustainable. For example, because farm machinery is powered by carbon-based fuels and petro-chemicals are necessary to kill pests and weeds and fertilize crops, large-scale farms are overly dependent on fossil fuels, such as oil, which are becoming increasingly expensive and will eventually be depleted. This dependence on fossil fuels also contributes to global warming at a time when many policymakers and experts say it is imperative to reduce greenhouse gas emissions. Critics say factory farming damages the environment in other ways, as well, because large crop fields and animal production facilities require massive amounts of land and water resources and they often produce air and water pollution due to the overuse of chemicals and the huge amounts of animal waste. In addition, these environmental effects have been linked to health problems in humans and wildlife. Many agricultural experts have concluded that agriculture must make another big transformation in the coming decades, a shift to a smaller, more environmentally friendly and sustainable model of farming. Supporters of industrial farm methods, however, maintain that factory methods are necessary to produce enough food to feed the world, and that crop and animal producers are constantly working to make improvements in the areas of animal welfare and environmental protection.

The authors of the viewpoints included in *Current Controversies: Factory Farming* illuminate some of the many different facets of the debate about factory farms—on issues such as whether factory farming is economically beneficial, whether it treats animals in an ethical way, whether it harms the environment or human health, and how it may have to change or adapt in the future.

CHAPTER 1

Is Factory Farming Economically Beneficial?

Chapter Preface

The U.S. model of large-scale animal production is rapidly being adopted by a number of developing countries, including Mexico, India, Argentina, Brazil, China, Pakistan, South Africa, Taiwan, Thailand, and nations that make up the former Soviet Union. This trend is being fueled, in part, by globalization. As developed countries such as those in Europe adopt and consider more stringent environmental and other regulations of meat producers, some large agribusiness corporations are moving their operations to less developed regions where environmental controls are much more lax. Also, the U.S. government has long promoted industrial agricultural development—such as the use of pesticides, synthetic fertilizers, and other chemicals and confined animal production—as part of its foreign aid and assistance to developing nations. Moreover, meat is viewed as a high-status food around the world, and as poor countries develop their economies and their citizens become more affluent, the demand for meat rises. In fact, global meat production has increased five-fold since 1950, and meat consumption is rising the fastest in the developing world. According to Worldwatch Institute, an independent research organization, up to two-thirds of the gains in meat consumption in recent years were in developing countries, which have turned to factory methods to boost their production of meat.

Like the United States, however, many developing countries are discovering that the factory farming of meat, while producing cheap and plentiful protein, brings with it a number of serious consequences. One such outcome is the costly environmental degradation that results when thousands of animals are kept together in close confinement. Large animals such as pigs, for example, can produce massive amounts of foul-smelling manure and liquid waste. Although manure makes good fertilizer in small amounts because it contains nitrogen and phosphorous, in high concentrations it becomes a toxic pollutant. This is clearly illustrated in North Carolina, where more than ten million hogs are raised and processed each year, and factory farms must cope with more than nineteen million tons of manure annually. Typically, these wastes are stored in big lagoons, but sometimes these lagoons leak into groundwater, and in the case of storms, can flood hundreds of acres of land and nearby waterways. In developing countries, if producers are less careful about the processing of animal wastes, the results can be devastating to the local environment.

Factory meat production also creates health issues for the people living in developing regions. Nearby residents must deal with the pollution created by such operations, which can cause respiratory and stomach ailments. In addition, workers hired in large-scale meat facilities situated in poorer countries typically have even fewer protections than their counterparts in the developed world, and conditions in animal operations and slaughterhouses can be quite hazardous. Not only are workers routinely in contact with sick and dying animals from whom they may catch diseases, but slaughterhouse workers also must stun and butcher animals at such a fast pace that they are at high risk for accidents.

Meanwhile, food-borne diseases are rampant in developing countries, and experts believe that the trend toward factory farming of animals is a leading cause. The crowded, unsanitary conditions at factory farms, combined with inadequate waste treatment, creates a perfect environment for animal diseases to spread to humans. The spread of the H1N1 virus, also known as swine flu, in 2009, for example, is believed by some experts to have originated in an industrial pig farm in Mexico. Food-borne infections, which can be spread from animals to humans when people eat food contaminated by animal manure, are another problem. Animals raised in close confinement often live and die in their own excrement, and developing countries typically have fewer safeguards to prevent the chance of contamination during slaughtering and processing.

The routine use of antibiotics in factory animal production is a cause for concern as well. Animals housed in crowded conditions are more prone to disease, so antibiotics are given to livestock to prevent disease and to increase growth. The problem, however, is that many of the same drugs that are used in animals also are used to treat human illnesses, and their widespread usage is causing dangerous microbes to develop resistance to many antibiotics, threatening human health.

Another consequence of factory farming in the developing world is that it can destroy traditional farming methods and threaten local animal breeds, bringing more instead of less poverty to poor nations. In many less developed regions, people still rely on small-scale, subsistence farming to make a living. Often, these small farm operations raise a variety of crops and animal breeds that are indigenous to the region. If an intensive meat production facility opens nearby, however, these small farmers often lose their livelihoods and are driven out of business because they simply cannot compete with the low prices achieved by intensive production methods. Formerly self-sufficient small farmers then become consumers, and they must find some other way to earn a living so they can afford to buy meat from the factory farms. In this way, factory farming can change whole societies and cultures.

This trend toward factory farming may not last, however. Increasingly, policymakers and world leaders are weighing whether the economic benefits of factory farming outweigh the environmental, health, and other costs. In 2001, for example, the World Bank, an international lending organization that has funded animal factory farm projects in the past, released a new livestock strategy that noted the various problems with large-scale livestock farms in developing nations and that promised to apply guidelines to livestock development projects that will reduce poverty, protect environmental sustainability, ensure food security and safety, and promote animal welfare. The authors of the viewpoints in this chapter offer their views on the critical question of whether factory farms are economically beneficial.

Modern Farming Techniques Are Essential to Provide Food to a Fast-Growing World Population

Chuck Jolley

Chuck Jolley is a freelance writer based in Kansas City, who covers a wide range of agriculture industry topics for Cattlenet work.com *and* Agnetwork.com. *He also is president and cofounder of the Meat Industry Hall of Fame (MIHOF), an organization created to honor leaders in the meat industry.*

I've always been fascinated by arguments framed by emotional issues. They reveal people's 'gut' reactions but often leave the real facts trampled in the dust. Slicksters from the political, religious and social arenas have always known they can stir the pot with appeals to the heart combined with callous dismissals of the 'science.' They enjoy a short time in the sun but soon show they've earned the label of snake oil salesmen.

It's an easy, too convenient way to win the public's opinion, maybe because we are such an emotional species and the science tends to be too dry and unemotional. So often, it's also the best way to lead the public down the wrong path; to lead them to the fork in the road and stand aside as they insist on taking the path most traveled, the familiar route that's seen as safer and less frightening.

And so it is with the issue of factory farming vs. family farming. With well over 90% of our population off the farm for several generations, the use of emotional appeals and loaded terms such as factory farms and 'big' food by groups such as HSUS [Humane Society of the United States] and PETA [People for the Ethical Treatment of Animals] have served to stampede public opinion and forced California style Proposition 2 laws [Proposition 2 is the Prevention of Farm Animal Cruelty Act, which was a California ballot measure adopted in 2008] on the ag [agricultural] community.

Changing Agricultural Laws

Here is a list of similar laws gleaned from *Wikipedia*:

- On November 5, 2002, Florida voters passed Amendment 10, an amendment to the Florida Constitution banning the confinement of pregnant pigs in gestation crates. The Amendment passed by a margin of 55% for and 45% against.

- On November 7, 2006, Arizona voters passed Proposition 204 with 62% support. The measure prohibits the confinement of calves in veal crates and breeding sows in gestation crates.

- On June 28, 2007, Oregon Governor Ted Kulongoski signed a measure into law prohibiting the confinement of pigs in gestation crates (SB 694, 74th Leg. Assembly, Regular Session).

- On May 14, 2008, Colorado Governor Bill Ritter signed into law a bill, SB 201, that phases out gestation crates and veal crates.

- Germany, Switzerland, Sweden, and Austria have all banned battery cages for egg-laying hens. The entire European Union is phasing out battery cages by 2012.

At a time when a fast-growing world population needs all the help it can get to deliver sufficient food resources, assailing 'factory' farms and urging a return to a nation of small family farms seems almost suicidal. The science points to the fact that modern farming techniques and the advances we've seen in agriculture in the past half century have almost completely eradicated the famines we've endured for millennia. . . .

So I went looking for someone who could speak eloquently for the science of modern food production—not someone with an obvious ax to grind or a glaring prejudice for or against big farms/family farms. I found her as I was researching the issue on the internet. She had made a comment on a food blog that seemed well-thought and calmly rational. I tracked her down and asked just the second question in the interview that follows. Her response was so intriguing, I asked her to expand on that thought.

An Expert Opinion

Here is Five Minutes with Cathy Bandyk:

Chuck Jolley: Let's start by establishing credentials. How did you get into agriculture?

Cathy Bandyk: I have had the opportunity to hold multiple roles in one agriculture industry, which I hope has helped me evaluate issues and situations with a broader view. I grew up in a rural town in northeast Kansas, and after completing my first degree in animal science from K-State [Kansas State University], my husband and I spent 15 years running a mixed crop and livestock operation on the edge of the Flint Hills. During that time I spent a year as a county agent, was program assistant for KSU's [Kansas State University's] International Grains Program, returned to graduate school to complete a PhD in ruminant nutrition, and worked as part of the KSU beef Extension team.

> *Individuals . . . have the opportunity in our free market to devote their personal resources to consumer choices that they consider "natural" or "sustainable."*

I have also had a side business focused on ration balancing software. For the last 9 years, I've been the cow/calf and stocker cattle nutritionist for Quality Liquid Feeds, responsible for training and technical support through much of the country. And like all of us I am a consumer, wanting safe, wholesome, and satisfying food on the table for my three sons.

Let me throw some phrases at you—all seemingly related: family farms, locavores, natural and organic foods, sustainable agriculture. Their common reference point is a small but growing movement that is rebelling against concepts like factory farming and industrial food production. What is the proper place for that movement and can it be relied on to help feed the world's millions of people living with what we now call food insecurity?

The simple answers to those apparently straight-forward questions are "niche" and "no," and they can be backed by facts and figures. But your comments leading up to the question are loaded with catch phrases that propel the discussion out of the realm of statistics and logic, and into the treacherous and powerful world of emotions.

Individuals whose impression of modern agriculture is based on the images generated by the term "factory farming" have the opportunity in our free market to devote their personal resources to consumer choices that they consider "natural" or "sustainable." Producers have the option to target this market niche, but make that choice needing and expecting higher prices for their goods to compensate for the increased costs of reduced efficiency.

Scientific and Technological Advances Are Necessary

But can we get to the heart of the issue? Can smaller agriculture units be relied on to feed the world's fast-growing population?

In the bigger picture, which is what the question directly asks, it is dangerous and irresponsible to imply we can provide adequate, safe, wholesome food to a growing world population while turning our backs on scientific and technological advances. Judicious application of our collective knowledge is the only way to supply all the equally deserving hungry mouths on the planet, and to take care of our world at the same time.

Which leads to the next logical question—'big' food vs 'slow' food; is 'big' the villain here?

Professional food production is marked by a commitment to continued improvement, and the information required to pursue that goal; informed husbandry decisions; acknowledged responsibility for long-term conservation of natural resources; consistent health and nutritional care; and, the availability of adequate resources—physical, human, and monetary—to support continuous utilization of all the tools available to efficiently and humanely convert limited natural resources into safe, high quality food.

As I travel the country, I see these principles embraced by operations that are big and not so big, and on both sides of the line drawn by someone's definition of "family farm."

Land Is a Limited Resource

What would happen if we returned to a less intensive agricultural model?

A widespread return to less intensive agriculture would result in a reduction in food availability, the conversion of additional acres to food production, or both. Land is our absolutely limited resource. Minimizing land needed for agricultural use allows more unique or sensitive ecosystems to be left for conservation or recreation; practices that yield less per acre necessitate tillage or grazing in those areas instead.

Efficiency truly is the key. And an important point that is frequently overlooked is that animal performance and efficiency are directly correlated to animal welfare. Commercial production practices were developed to meet both these goals concurrently.

One of the growing attitudes about animal agriculture is that farm animals are needlessly restrained and mistreated. Folks involved in organizations like HSUS and PETA have been successful in getting laws passed that have outlawed farrowing crates, for instance. What would be the long term effect if those laws become more widespread?

Farmers, ranchers and animal scientists all know that anything—environment, social interaction, health or nutritional status—that stresses livestock will result in lowered gains, reproduction, and feed conversion. Management decisions are geared to minimize stress, for the good of both the animals and the operation's economic sustainability. Allowing government policy to override experience and science because the public has been led to view animal experience from a human perspective can actually do more harm than good.

An example from my personal past: having sadly fished flattened piglets out of an open pen, I see farrowing crate use as an opportunity to better tend to the animals in my care, not as an act of cruelty! Yet a growing number of entities—with diverse intentions and agendas—are bent on making these distinctions and decisions for us. As someone who is personally and professionally dedicated to science-based and responsible stewardship and food production, I find this trend disturbing, if not actually frightening.

Modern Animal Agriculture Methods Are Efficient, Highly Productive, and Sustainable

Animal Agriculture Alliance

Animal Agriculture Alliance is an organization that promotes the interests of some of the largest corporations and trade associations in the business of animal livestock, animal drugs, genetically engineered foods and crops, and other related issues.

On the heels of an announcement by the United Nations Chief stating food price increases have led to a global crisis, the Union of Concerned Scientists (UCS) is proposing that farmers move away from food animal production systems that allow plentiful production of meat, milk and eggs. The UCS prefers that we move to systems requiring more land mass; which expose our animals to dangers including inclement weather conditions, predators, and disease; which could lead to more carbon emissions and limit the amount of food that can be produced for the world.

Yesterday's Agriculture

In 1900, the population of the United States was about one-fourth of what it is today (76 million in 1900; 303+ million in 2008). The number of people involved in food production has gone from nearly 100 percent of the population producing at least some (if not all) of the food their families consumed in the early 1900s to less than two percent of the population producing food for everyone.

Here are some facts about today's consumers and animal agriculture:

- The American population is growing an average of one percent per year. Domestic and global per capita consumption of meat, milk and eggs is increasing rapidly.

- Exports are on the rise: in 1960 the U.S. exported 161,306 tons of meat; in 2006 the U.S. exported 4,572,409 tons of meat.

- The number of producers has drastically decreased while the number of animals producing milk, meat and eggs has drastically increased. This has been necessary because livestock prices have not kept up with inflation, forcing the need to consolidate operations and produce more animals to stay economically viable as a business.

In the 1950s most food animal production was "free-range"—the same type of production system the UCS prefers for all involved in animal agriculture. Here is a view of what was common under free-range production systems:

- Animals were raised outdoors which did not allow for farmers to protect them from:

- Extreme heat, cold, wind, rain, snow, hail, etc.

- Dirty conditions

- Predators

- Disease and parasites

- The animals' diets were much less controlled. Because animals' food intake was poorly regulated (it was routine for animals to be fed scraps or forced to live off of the land), the food product attributes were not consistent, nor controllable.

- Veterinarians and producers had a much more difficult job monitoring and maintaining the health of the animals because of the lack of environmental control.

- In 1947–1951, humans contracted a median of 395 cases of trichinosis (including 57 deaths) largely as a result of consuming pork. This was because pigs were routinely fed scraps and were exposed to wildlife. With production changes, from 1997–2001 there was a median of 12 cases of trichinosis annually (none of which resulted in death); the vast majority of these cases is attributable to consumption of wild animal meat.

Modern production practices allow animals to produce food that is consistent in quality and attributes.

Today's Agriculture

In contrast, today's food animal production systems are much more sophisticated and produce a much higher quality food product. Here are some of the other positive outcomes of today's systems:

- Animals are housed in barns which allow animal caretakers to constantly monitor herd health, ensure the comfort of the animals, keep the animals clean and protect the animals from predators, disease and extreme weather.

- Animals are fed carefully formulated diets that meet their nutritional needs and ensure a quality food product that meets the characteristics consumers demand.

- Animals are provided with the best care possible through the advice of veterinarians. Animal health products are provided to animals to prevent, control and treat disease as well as ensure nutritional efficacy. Because the animals' environment is sustained, this job is easier for both producers and veterinarians. . . .

Should legislative changes force the food animal industry to change its production methods to those that were commonplace decades ago, we can expect to face many of the challenges we have overcome in the past. Here are some specific examples of how the world may look:

- Most importantly, the current food crisis will get much bleaker. The move away from modern production systems in exchange for those of yesteryear would be a monumental setback in food production. It could equate to major food shortages and outrageous food prices.

- Exposing food animals to uncontrollable factors in the natural environment could lead to transmission of disease like avian influenza (bird flu) which could then be transmitted to the general population.

- The quality of meat, milk and eggs could decline significantly. Modern production practices allow animals to produce food that is consistent in quality and attributes. Shifting to systems which take away variation in the animals' diet and care also take away the ability to ensure a consistent, quality food product.

It is with great concern that the Animal Agriculture Alliance Coalition urges these points to be considered prior to making legislative mandates that do not consider the implications on the needs and welfare of the entire consuming public.

U.S. Dairy Farmers Are Feeding the World by Producing Quality Foods

Pam Taylor

Pam Taylor is a reporter for the Minnesota Women's Press, *a newspaper devoted to issues and events that affect women's lives from a feminist perspective.*

"I love cows!" Barb Liebenstein said. "I love their behavior. I love the challenge of getting them to help me do my job. How can your day be bad when you start by walking past your calves—the future of your business—and see those beautiful faces? That's when this job gets pretty easy."

Liebenstein's job? Running the Wolf Creek Dairy. She is co-owner/operator of the Dundas, Minn., farming business with her husband, Paul. Wolf Creek is one of two independently owned dairy farms left in Bridgewater Township, 40 miles south of the Twin Cities.

"Fifty years ago there were hundreds of dairies in our area and now there are two. I guess we'd better be doing a good job if we want this to last," she said.

A Thing for Animals

Working in a family business with a spouse for a partner is something Liebenstein learned about when she was growing up. Her parents were role models for her as they worked together in their greenhouse business near Virginia, Minn. Liebenstein and her sister, Deb, worked with them, helping to grow bedding plants—annuals and perennials—and sod. "[My parents] treated each other with respect," she said. "And, they taught us also that you need to take time for yourself.

"Deb and I grew up driving tractors," Liebenstein said, "but I wanted to get as far away from [greenhouse work] as I could." She had inherited a love of animals, especially horses, from her father. While her sister is now the third generation to own the family greenhouse business, Liebenstein said, "I just wasn't cut out to work with plants. Living, breathing animals are just more my thing." She went to the University of Minnesota-Waseca to become a veterinary technician, with the goal of working with large animals.

After completing her degree, Liebenstein worked for five years at a Northfield [Minnesota] veterinary clinic. It was during this time that she met her future husband, Paul, a dairy farmer. After they married, in addition to milking cows, she continued on her own career path in the oncology department at the University of Minnesota College of Veterinary Medicine.

In 1994, after her husband needed two back surgeries due to the physical strain of farm work, Liebenstein joined in his dream of a larger-scale, more sustainable dairy business. The farm grew from "40 cows to 300 almost overnight. It was exciting, scary, crazy," she said. She uses her veterinary technician skills on a daily basis, explaining that farmers don't just milk cows, they care for them and work hard to keep them healthy.

With six full-time and six part-time employees milking cows in three shifts daily, Liebenstein admits there were days when her own daughters thought the farm came first in their lives. "We all work together, probably more than our daughters would like." Her daughters, Grace, a first-year student at South Dakota State University, and Mary, a ninth-grader at Northfield High School, have active roles on the farm and each has her own animals to care for. Liebenstein is proud of her daughters' strong sense of self and not feeling intimidated or out of place in the dairy industry.

Feeding the World

Liebenstein is passionate about taking care of cows and producing quality milk. "As a woman and a mother, I take pride in creating a healthy environment for our cows and our employees," she said. "Our mission statement is to 'provide a good quality of life for ourselves, our employees, our cows and the environment.'"

[Farmers] don't want to be seen as . . . villain[s] when we're applying education and technology to do the best job that we can.

Wolf Creek Dairy is now home to 400 black and white Holsteins that produce 4,000 gallons of milk each day. Some of that milk is made into cheese that is "sold everywhere. We are feeding the world from here," Liebenstein said.

The average-sized dairy farm in Minnesota is 106 cows. Big farms have 1,500 to 2,000 cows. She considers Wolf Creek Dairy to be a middle-sized farm. According to the Midwest Dairy Association, there are 5,100 dairy farms in Minnesota today. "Even if the horizon is scary for the farming industry," Liebenstein said, "we will be just fine as long as we stay focused on what is important."

Getting the message out about farming practices is important to Liebenstein. Whether large scale or small, she is concerned about the perception the public has about farmers.

"We really care and are really passionate about the job that we do," she said. "We look at it as feeding the world." She often finds herself in the roles of being an educator and a defender of dairy farming, due to misconceptions from terms such as "factory farms." "I don't want to be seen as a villain when we're applying education and technology to do the best job that we can."

Liebenstein is concerned about the disconnect people have with where food comes from—and how a farm works. She gives tours to help people understand.

My No. 1 priority is taking care of our environment.

"We have tours here all the time," Liebenstein said, hosting school groups, dairy industry meetings, politicians who have never been on a farm before, even royalty from India. Last June she invited her whole community and had 500 people visit for a "Day on the Farm." "I never turn anyone down for a tour."

"My No. 1 priority is taking care of our environment," Liebenstein said, "leaving something better for our kids." As she reflected on her life on a farm, she said, "When I walk out my door and get to see those calves every morning on the way out to my office, it is pretty neat. On a day like today," she continued, "all is right with the world . . . [feeling like you're] doing a really good job, taking care of cows, making sure you're making a quality product—at the end of the day, it's so rewarding."

It Is a Myth That Industrialized Agriculture Produces Cheap Food to Feed the World

Lenny Russo

Lenny Russo is currently the chef and proprietor of Heartland Contemporary Midwestern Restaurant & Wine Bar in St. Paul, Minnesota.

As a chef and restaurateur, a great deal of my world revolves around food. Consequently, I spend much of my time thinking about it. That includes the quality, availability and cost of the food I need to continue to operate a profitable business. As it concerns my restaurant, that rarely involves my looking at the commodities market.

The commodities market report informs us of the current prices of various food stuffs including but not limited to fruits, vegetables, grains, meat, eggs and dairy products. The report includes both conventionally and organically grown foods. It has only peripheral bearing on what I do since I buy directly from farmers, many of whom don't sell their products on the commodities market and subsequently don't base their prices on it. It does affect me to the extent that some of my local flour and grains are traded in that way and also to the extent that some of my farmers don't raise their own feed and are subject in that regard to price fluctuations as they impact their production costs.

A Better Food System

At Heartland [Russo's restaurant in St. Paul, Minnesota], we practice fair trade. In other words, we ask that our farmers make themselves aware of what it costs for them to get their

Lenny Russo, "The Myth of Cheap Food," Startribune.com, June 27, 2009. Reproduced by permission of the author.

product to market and to pay themselves the equivalent of a living wage. By that we mean they should be able to charge enough in order to be profitable to the extent that they can put a roof over their heads, send their kids to school, obtain necessary health care, feed and clothe themselves and put a little away for retirement. Should their production costs increase, we expect for them to charge us more for their product. Should they see their costs go down, we ask that they pass some of the savings on to us. It's a partnership built on trust and goodwill as opposed to speculation on a trading floor.

A few weeks ago [2009], I wrote about what I consider to be our broken food system. I proposed that when based upon a fair trade system like the one we use at Heartland, creating a more efficient conduit for distribution of locally and sustainably grown food would help lower the production costs thereby enabling our local farmers to be more competitive in the marketplace. In turn, that would allow for greater accessibility to more healthful and flavorful foods to a larger demographic and consequently benefit us all by not only boosting the local economy but also in improving the health and well being of both the community and the environment as well as improving the quality of life for many of us.

This may be the only time in history when we in America are overfed and under nourished.

In response, one commenter to this blog insisted I was uneducated in the physiology of plants first by claiming that the essential fatty acids known as omega-3's cannot be produced by plants. He later recanted that claiming he was a bit intoxicated when he responded and then claimed that he was referring to omega-6 fatty acids. Of course, he was wrong on both accounts. In fact, the human body is incapable of producing those essential fats and must acquire them through the consumption of food stuffs. If vegetarians and especially vegans were unable to obtain these fats from plants, they would die. He also claimed that I was a shill for corporate America which is probably the furthest thing from which I am. I only mention this because another claim he made was that suggesting that we buy locally and sustainably produced food simply because it tastes better is folly since it costs way too much to produce. Again, he missed the point entirely. First of all, it is not just about taste; it is about nutrition as well. Part of the reason more nutritious food tastes better is because nature has intended it to be that way so that we will be inclined to feed ourselves in a more nutritionally efficient manner. As far as the cost is concerned, that was pretty much my point. Let's create a system that helps reduce the cost so that we may all have a better quality of life.

There is no such thing as cheap food.

The Myth of Cheap Food

That brings me to what I call the "myth of cheap food". We hear it being bandied about all the time. That is, the claim that through the miracles of modern technology that we have made it possible to produce enormous amounts of cheap food and thereby feed the world. In fact, this may be the only time in history when we in America are overfed and under nourished. Instead of growing nutrient rich vegetable crop, our farms have been growing vast amounts of feed corn and soybeans which are respectively enormous reservoirs of cheap calories and protein. Never mind that these genetically modified crops are being grown in nutrient deficient soil that produces nutrient deficient plants to be consumed by us who are then by consequence nutrient deficient. We sure are able to afford to get a belly full of it. Just look around at the expanding waistlines of the over sized population if you don't believe me. For some reason, we hardly ever hear about this as being one of the terrible things we have done to ourselves in the names of profit and the so-called advancement of science.

Here is a simple biological fact to assist in putting it in perspective for you. A nerve cell, or neuron, runs on glucose which is sugar. It is the fuel it needs to function properly. Once a neuron has absorbed all of what it needs, the rest of that sugar is still floating around in the bloodstream where the body converts it to triglycerides which, as many of us know, are fats. All of this excess sugar that people consume in the form of highly processed foods, including things as simple as a loaf of factory made supermarket bread, is still floating around waiting for this conversion to happen. Those fats and sugars are contributing to the vast increases we see in the onset of obesity, heart disease, high blood pressure and type-2 diabetes. We sure may feel full when eat that super sized fast food meal, but we remain nutritionally deficient.

So here is what I am saying. There is no such thing as cheap food. It's a myth that is perpetuated by a huge propaganda machine that has convinced us that we are doing the best we can for ourselves by continuing to eat garbage. The fact is that we can pay for our food up front at the cash register when we choose to buy the most nutritionally complete whole foods we can find, or we can settle up on the back end at the doctor's office or in the pharmacy or at the hospital when the piper finally shows up to get paid. Don't even get me started on what it costs us taxpayers to clean up an environment that has been degraded by the abuses inherent in conventional farming practices. In the first scenario, we can choose to lead longer and healthier lives. In the second scenario, we can count to the end of our days wondering what's taking so long. The choice is ours.

Factory-Farmed, Meat-Based Diets May Cause a Food Scarcity Crisis

Jim Motavalli

Jim Motavalli is the editor of E/The Environmental Magazine, *an online magazine that focuses on environmental issues.*

It's important to look at the American way of producing and consuming meat, because it is, increasingly, a model for the rest of the world. Despite numerous health advisories, from the American Cancer Society to the American Dietary Association, that counsel consumers to limit their intake of high-fat animal protein, U.S. per capita consumption of beef and pork has steadily risen since 1970, and poultry consumption has almost tripled. A record 8.5 billion chickens were slaughtered in 1997 alone.

Diet is also firmly established as a leading factor in cancer risk: Dr. Walter Willett of Harvard's Departments of Nutrition and Epidemiology cites more than 200 studies that suggest there is a reduced cancer risk in people who cut back on animal products and eat plenty of fruits and vegetables. And while we may have come to believe that heart disease is a natural and expected end to life, the incidence of this number one killer of Americans is much lower in countries that adhere to a low-fat diet with minimal animal products. Alan Durning, director of Northwest Environmental Watch, puts it simply, "If you think about individual lifestyle choices Americans can make, eating less meat should be in the top 10." Currently, the Chinese have only five percent of the heart disease risk of western societies, but those figures are likely to change as the Chinese diet increasingly resembles our own. . . .

Jim Motavali, "The Trouble with Meat," Emagazine.com, 2009. Reproduced by permission.

Meat production in China, which experienced a 40 percent jump in per capita income between 1990 and 1994, has risen faster than anywhere else in the world. China, the most populous country in the world, now accounts for a quarter of the world's production and consumption of meat. Last year, China's Xinhua news agency reported that there are 1,000 foreign or joint-venture meat processing projects underway in the country. "Extensive international cooperation is needed to push the meat industry to a new stage of development," said Vice Minister of Internal Trade He Jihai at a world meat conference in Beijing. . . .

Western-Style Problems

But that "new stage" of intensive agriculture may bring with it some western-style problems. Last December, the government of Hong Kong ordered the slaughter of more than one million chickens, the former colony's whole population, after a strain of influenza virus killed four people. Eighty percent of Hong Kong's poultry comes from farms in mainland China.

Dr. Robert Lawrence, one of the founders of the Center for a Livable Future at Johns Hopkins University in Baltimore, puts an ironic twist on an old dinner table admonishment. Instead of telling kids to eat all their food because of "the starving children in China," the modern version is, "Don't put all that food on your plate—think of all the starving future generations."

The notion that a period of food scarcity might be ahead, and that our wasteful, unhealthy, factory-farmed, meat-based diet is at the root of the problem, provided the impetus for the new center's founding last year. Dr. Polly Walker, the center's director, compares the task of changing people's diets to that of getting Americans to recycle. "Recycling didn't change the standard of living, but it changed the way people did things," she says. "It was assumed then that Americans would never clean and sort their containers, but now it's a natural part of living."

Walker sees the center's work as "getting at the nexis of consumption, environment, land use and modern farming methods. The purpose is to affect policy and change public opinion." To that end, the center held its first conference, "Equity, Health and the Earth's Resources: Food Security and Social Justice," at the school last November [2008]. In a talk entitled, "What is a Healthy Diet?" Dr. T. Colin Campbell of Cornell University discussed his work with The China Health Project, which has studied the diets of Chinese peasants since the early 1980s. His conclusion: the more plant-based foods in the diet, the lower the incidence of disease. "The Chinese who eat the least fat and animal products have substantially lower rates of cancer, heart attack and several other chronic, degenerative diseases," Dr. Campbell says. Ironically, Chinese cities are trying to play catch up with the west: Shanghai, for instance, has Kentucky Fried Chicken, Pizza Hut and McDonald's.

A global switch to meat-based diets and factory farming methods is very much an environmental issue.

While it's not an animal rights group, the center concludes that modern intensive animal agriculture methods "harm animals unnecessarily and produce food inefficiently." Henry Spira, the veteran activist who is coordinator of Animal Rights International in New York, says the center's work "is important because it focuses on solving problems," he says. "It's not just a bunch of academics talking. It's a think tank, but also a 'do' tank."

An Environmental Issue

A global switch to meat-based diets and factory farming methods is very much an environmental issue, both because of widespread land degradation as a result of overgrazing and the increasing diversion of world grain supplies and produc-

tive farm land to feed a burgeoning population of domesti-
cated animals. China, for instance, fed 17 percent of its grain
to livestock in 1985; by 1994, that figure had risen to 23 percent. In the U.S.—the model—70 percent of the grain produced is fed to animals. As Dr. Robert Lawrence of the new
Johns Hopkins Center for a Livable Future points out, "The
inefficiency of converting eight or nine kilograms of grain
protein into one kilogram of animal protein for human consumption would by itself be sufficient argument against continuation of our present dietary habits."

---

*Americans will probably be eating far less meat and
dairy products by 2050.*

Lester Brown of The Worldwatch Institute, whose report
on likely grain shortages in China caused an international fu-
ror in 1996, says, "What's happening in China teaches us that,
despite rising affluence, our likely world population of 10 billion people won't be able to live as high on the food chain as
the average American. There simply won't be enough food.
Much of the animal overgrazing we first reported in a 1991
paper is worse now than it was then. The pressures on the
world's rangelands are more serious than those on oceanic
fisheries. We're pushing our natural systems to their limits and
beyond, with the likely result that we'll see the growing im-
poverishment of rural areas."

It isn't only developing countries that may be forced to re-
verse the current world trend toward heavier meat consumption. Brown's position is bolstered by a 1995 report from the
American Association for the Advancement of Science, which
said that Americans will probably be eating far less meat and
dairy products by 2050. U.S. croplands, the report said, have
reached the limits of production, even as the U.S. population
is projected to double in 50 years. The result, says association
member David Pimentel of Cornell University, is that the U.S.

could cease to be a food exporter by 2025, and the American diet, now 31 percent animal products, could drop to only 15 percent.

In 1996, the World Food Summit in Rome took a decidedly pessimistic tone about world food production, warning of an "unthinkable Malthusian nightmare" if global output is not doubled in the next 30 years to meet an expanding population and an increasing demand for meat. According to the British Independent, more than 800 million people do not get enough food to meet their basic needs, and 82 countries—half of them in Africa—neither grow enough food for their population nor can afford to import it.

Waste and Danger

China may be developing U.S.-style factory farming, but such intensive methods are still unknown in the Third World, where raising animals for slaughter is a much more haphazard affair. Dar Es Salaam, Tanzania, for instance, has no slaughterhouse at all, and animals are usually killed by meat vendors themselves, often under totally unhygienic conditions. Tanzania's agricultural ministry has warned of outbreaks of typhoid, cholera and tuberculosis if uncontrolled slaughter continues.

Cattle, sheep and goats graze half of the planet's land area, which is increasingly becoming depleted as a result. The United Nations estimates that more than 70 percent of the world's eight billion acres of dry range land is at least moderately desertified. As Worldwatch reports, persistent grazing makes bare ground impermeable to rain, which then runs off, carrying topsoil with it. The picture is not much better in wetter regions, because cattle have to compete with farmers and are crowded into small areas, accelerating erosion and degradation.

Another major problem is animal wastes, which wash off farms and into rivers and streams, polluting everything from groundwater in the Czech Republic to the Chesapeake Bay. In the U.S., years of dumping hog waste into North Carolina rivers has led to the bizarre spectacle of Pfiesteria piscicida, a seemingly innocuous phytoplankton that, in the presence of phosphates from nutrient-rich wastes, turns into voracious "flagellated vegetative cells" that kill fish and are extremely toxic to humans. . . .

Factory Farming and Disease

Criticism of factory farming has come from animal rights groups that emphasize its inhumane aspects. But, as Nicols Fox meticulously documents in her new book, *Spoiled: The Dangerous Truth About a Food Chain Gone Haywire*, the conditions on factory farms are tailor-made incubators for disease.

The modern broiler chicken house, Fox says, is no quaint little farm building, but a poultry metropolis holding up to 70,000 genetically similar birds in close confinement. "There is every evidence that Salmonella and E. coli don't have one cause but many, many causes," she says. "Any stress exacerbates the presence of microbes in chickens. And dirty water, dirty food, all of these things have been shown to increase the presence of pathogenic microorganisms, which spread much more quickly through flocks that are essentially clones of each other." In March, *Consumer Reports* revealed that its own testing had found Campylobacter in 63 percent of randomly selected chickens, and Salmonella in 13 percent. Only 29 percent of the birds tested were free of either bacteria. Almost all were infected with generic E. coli.

The Cato Institute's Jerry Taylor denies that cleaning up the meat industry will slow the spread of E. coli and Salmonella since, he believes, these recent strains "have absolutely zip to do with the food system." But Fox cites the example of Sweden, which has virtually eliminated Salmonella and drastically cut rates of Campylobacter infection through a strict hygienic regimen that includes rigidly controlled cleanliness for workers and the emptying, cleaning, disinfecting and sealing of hen houses after birds are sent to slaughter. Sweden also prohibits the use of antibiotics as a growth promoter. By killing other bacteria in chickens, Fox writes, commonly used poultry antibiotics can actually create an opportunity for Campylobacter or Salmonella to invade.

The animal waste problem is also a factory farming byproduct. One chicken house can process 1.5 million birds a week, and release 1.6 million gallons of wastewater per day. In one month in 1996, the state of Missouri had more hog manure spills and resulting fish kills than had occurred from all farming operations in the state in the past 10 years. Wastes once stayed on the farm, where they were used as manure. But, says Fox, "industrial meat companies are not farms so they don't recycle wastes. It ends up in the ecosystem, creating enormous problems."

Speed-Up on the Slaughterhouse Floor

Even if we fully adopted Sweden's methods, and our factory farms became as clean as hospitals, disease would still be rife in our meat supply. The reason can be found in the next stop in the modern farming assembly line: the slaughterhouse.

Animal slaughter has become a multinational business. In 1980, according to the U.S. Department of Agriculture (USDA), it took 53 companies with 103 plants to slaughter two-thirds of the country's cattle; by 1992, only three firms were doing the work in just 29 plants. Between 1984 and 1994, some 2,000 small slaughterhouses were driven out of business. The remaining mega-companies, many of them carrying big debt loads after consolidation, needed to maximize profits, and they did it by reducing workforces and speeding up the kill line. Factory workers say that inadequately stunned animals regularly run wild in slaughterhouses, endangering line employees, who either look the other way at food safety violations or lose their jobs.

According to Gail Eisnitz, author of the 1997 book *Slaughterhouse*, the other thing that fell by the wayside as the line cranked up was meat inspection. Eisnitz, who interviewed many slaughterhouse workers and federal meat inspectors, some of whom lost their jobs for talking to her, says, "The Humane Slaughter Act, while still on the books, has basically been repealed. Meat inspectors are not allowed to stop the line for violations—even though the law requires it—because their supervisors won't allow it. The inspectors I talked to went on the record and said that the regulations are just pieces of paper that they're unable to enforce. Deadly, contaminated meat is just pouring out of those plants, and I have the documentation to prove it."

The meat inspectors lost their power as part of the Reagan administration's deregulatory fervor. As Eisnitz reports, until the early 1980s, USDA poultry inspectors looked for contaminants like feces (a major source of E. coli infection), scabs and sores. Deregulation gave contamination responsibility to the workers; inspectors were reduced to looking for actual disease, which drastically curtailed their justification for stopping the line. The result, as the *Atlanta Journal Constitution* reported, is that millions of chickens "leaking yellow pus, stained by green feces, contaminated by harmful bacteria, or marred by lung and heart infections, cancerous tumors or skin conditions, are shipped for sale to consumers." Since Upton Sinclair's stomach-churning, legislation-inducing novel *The Jungle*, "things have only gotten worse," says Eisnitz.

Efficiency and Affluence

Given the horrific details, why would the rest of the world want to imitate American factory farming and slaughter methods? The simple answer is that our system is remarkably efficient. Worldwatch reports some basic arithmetic. In 1991, China had two billion chickens, but these farm-raised birds took as much as four times as long to reach marketable weights as U.S. poultry. "Thus at any given instant, China has more chickens than the United States, but during a year's time, the U.S. raises and slaughters three times as many," says Worldwatch. As populations increase, so does the need to produce more food to feed them, and increasingly the people's choice—influenced by America's overwhelming cultural pull—is meat.

"Meat is a symbol of affluence, and it becomes an addiction and a habit," says Henry Spira, coordinator of Animal Rights International. He compares meat to tobacco, and believes that a "weight of evidence" will eventually steer people away from animal products as it is beginning to do with cigarettes. "It's bad news for your health and the environment, and it needs to be deglamorized," he adds. That obviously hasn't happened yet. . . .

For most people, a meat-centered diet is still the easiest, least-complicated choice, but it may not remain so. If Nicols Fox can write a line like, "If there were a contest for the most contaminated product Americans bring into their kitchens, poultry would win hands down" and not get taken to court by all 13 states with food disparagement laws, perhaps she's on to something. But Fox wasn't just talking. In 1995, a USDA baseline study on contamination of chickens found "greater than 99 percent of broiler chicken carcasses had detectable E. coli." Add in the grim predictions about the future of the world grain supply and the loss of global grazing land, and the switch to meat could be stalled before it ever really gets off the ground.

Factory Farms Are Not More Efficient or Economically Beneficial than Conventional Family Farms

William J. Weida

William J. Weida is a professor of economics and business at The Colorado College, Colorado Springs, Colorado.

Proponents of factory farming claim factory farms and Concentrated Animal Feeding Operations (CAFOs) they often employ provide economic, social, and other benefits that do not accrue to conventional farms. These claims carry with them unstated assumptions. If the assumptions are not satisfied, these claims are likely to be incorrect. . . .

Assumptions About CAFOs

A review of the unstated assumptions of CAFO operation shows many are routinely violated by CAFO operators to increase profits. For example, the CAFO industry claims many benefits accrue from the use of liquid animal manure as a crop nutrient. This claim rests on the assumption that liquid manure is applied to the land at agronomic rates—rates that adequately nourish the crops without providing more fertilizer than crops can use. However, a 2003 study by the USDA [U.S. Department of Agriculture] found many CAFO owners knowingly over-applied liquid manure to lands closest to their operations to reduce the transportation costs of moving heavy tanks of liquid to distant fields. By over applying manure close to the CAFO and reducing hauling distances the CAFO owners increased their profits, but over-application violates the fundamental assumption underlying nutrient management

William J. Weida, "Considering the Rationales for Factory Farming," March 5, 2004, pp. 1–11. http://www.sraproject.org. Reproduced by permission of the author.

and in this instance it invalidates claims that applying liquid manure to crop land is a beneficial practice.

Among the many assumptions violated by the CAFO industry is the most basic assumption of all—that CAFOs and factory farms are agricultural enterprises. If this assumption is invalid, CAFOs should be regarded as industrial enterprises and should be subject to industrial regulation of their pollution. Because regulation as an industry would force CAFOs to spend money to clean up their operations and reduce their pollution, substantial resources are expended by the agriculture industry to keep consumers, regulators, legislators and the residents of rural regions from questioning this fundamental assumption—even though it is demonstrably invalid. In terms of scale of operations, levels of emitted pollution, and production characteristics, CAFOs are clearly industrial entities. The fact that the CAFO industry uses animals does not make it an agricultural enterprise any more than the fact that Ford uses iron in its automobiles makes it a mining enterprise.

Stacked on this invalid fundamental assumption is a large collection of additional assumptions—each of which is critical to some benefit claimed by factory farms. Some of these assumptions are required to support the theories and methodologies behind CAFOs and some simply arise from a desire to perpetuate the way we have been taught to view agriculture or the way it operates.

The CAFO industry realizes these assumptions are critical to maintaining an agricultural image. Money and effort are continuously expended to create a picture of industrial agricultural production that agrees with the consumer's preconceived assumptions about agriculture. For example, advertisements show hogs in meadows instead of concrete-floored sheds, dairy cows are pictured in grass instead of mud and feces, and chickens always appear to be outside in barnyards instead of crammed into huge poultry barns or battery cages.

The industry's unstated fear is obvious—if consumers realize what is really going on, purchases of the product will fall.

It is in this light that the assumptions underlying the claims of factory farming are considered.

The Claims and Critical Assumptions of Factory Farming

Many costs of CAFOs are shifted to their neighbors and their host region through air and water pollution.

Claims About Efficiency and Price

1. Claim: CAFOs enjoy economies of scale that allow efficiencies from standardization, specialization and concentration of productive resources.

   Necessary Assumption: The average cost of producing a pound of meat continues to drop as CAFOs become larger.

   Reality: CAFOs only confine animals in less space, they do nothing to reduce the amount of land needed to raise feed for the animals and they do nothing to reduce the amount of land ultimately needed to recycle the animal waste. Costs stop declining as CAFOs get larger because the cost of waste disposal for a CAFO increases sharply after one surpasses the ability of the land to absorb the waste.

   Result: CAFOs try to avoid paying their increasing costs by shifting them to the surrounding region. While the CAFO may be successful in doing this, the confined operation is still less efficient in an economic sense.

2. Claim: Economies of scale gained from size and mechanization enable CAFOs to produce cheap food.

> Necessary Assumption: The price of food produced in CAFOs reflects all the costs involved in their production.
>
> Reality: Many costs of CAFOs are shifted to their neighbors and their host region through air and water pollution. These costs are not paid by the CAFO, thereby increasing its profit.
>
> Result: The price of food does not reflect its true cost and more food tends to be purchased, consumed and wasted because it is valued too cheaply. This results in a misallocation of national resources and leaves the bill for pollution cleanup with taxpayers in the state or region where the CAFO is located.

3. Claim: Cheap food saves consumers money.

> Necessary Assumption: The sticker price of food is the only cost paid by consumers.
>
> Reality: Many costs of CAFOs are shifted to others through air and water pollution which cause increased medical costs and increased tax costs for control and remediation. These costs are not paid by the CAFO and are not included in the price of CAFO produced food.
>
> Result: The price of food does not reflect its true cost to the consumer. When additional costs of pollution are added, the real costs of food rise. Individuals who consume the food may not pay these costs, but the costs are paid by society as a whole.

4. Claim: With free trade, surplus agricultural production from CAFOs in the US and Canada can simply be ex-

ported to other countries. This allows the price farmers receive for agricultural goods to remain high.

Necessary Assumptions: (1) David Ricardo, the economist who developed the theory of free trade assumed the factors of production (land, labor, capital) would not be exported to other countries. (2) The US and Canada produce agricultural products more efficiently relative to other goods (such as manufactured goods) than their competitors. (3) The US and Canada operate under the same environmental and business regulations as their competitors in the export markets.

Reality: Factors of production are regularly exported to areas of cheap labor, cheap feed, and poor regulation. US and Canadian production are only more efficient relative to other kinds of production if the costs of the pollution they generate are not considered. Neither the US nor Canada has a comparative advantage in labor-intensive activities and this forces both countries to resort to an industrial model of agricultural production to remain competitive in the global export market. However, because pollution regulation is often poor in export competitor nations, this industrial model is only competitive if environmental regulation is lax. As a result, producers who continue to operate in the US and Canada choose to locate their operations in regions with the poorest environmental regulation.

Result: Agriculture has only two ways to compete: (1) adopt a complete industrial model without industrial pollution regulation and then shift the costs of their operations to others or (2) rely on massive government subsidies to feed producers and CAFO operators. Most US and Canadian operators benefit from both methods of operation. Subsidies lower the cost of food consumed in importing countries (at the expense of US and Canadian taxpayers) and pollution cost shifting lowers the cost of food consumed in importing countries at the expense of rural residents and regions where CAFOs are located. To sustain this system, there is considerable pressure in both countries to relax environmental regulations and increase subsidy payments.

Claims About the CAFO's Place in Agriculture

5. Claim: Agriculture is the traditional method by which rural economies have run and factory farms are a logical continuation of this tradition and lifestyle.

> Necessary Assumption: Factory farms employ the same practices as traditional agriculture and if they create problems, those problems are of the same type and scale as those created by traditional agriculture.
>
> Reality: CAFOs are industries not agriculture. They create industrial-sized pollution and waste problems. They masquerade as agriculture because pollution monitoring and pollution regulation are weaker in the agricultural sector.
>
> Result: The regulatory structure, enforcement capabilities, and governing infrastructure of rural areas operate under the assumption they are dealing with agricultural problems. They are incapable of adequately dealing with large factory farms. As a result, CAFOs are largely allowed to shift the pollution costs of their operations to the rural region in which they reside.

CHAPTER 2

Is Factory Farming an Ethical Way to Treat Animals?

Chapter Preface

The only federal law that protects farm animals is the Humane Methods of Livestock Slaughter Act (HMLSA). First enacted in 1958, the HMLSA requires that animals be rendered insensible to pain before they are slaughtered to ensure a quick, painless death. The law also sets forth the specific methods of slaughtering and handling deemed to be humane:

> In the case of cattle, calves, horses, mules, sheep, swine, and other livestock, all animals are rendered insensible to pain by a single blow or gunshot or an electrical, chemical or other means that is rapid and effective, before being shackled, hoisted, thrown, cast, or cut.[1]

However, the HMLSA contains a broad exemption for slaughtering done in accordance with religious laws. The Act was updated in 1978 to give inspectors from the U.S. Department of Agriculture (USDA) enforcement authority, and further improvements in enforcement were made in 2002 when farm legislation included a resolution that the HMLSA should be fully enforced.

The most commonly used methods of slaughter are electrocution and carbon dioxide gassing for swine and captive bolt stunning for cattle, sheep, horses, and goats. Captive bolt stunning shoots a bolt, propelled by a blank cartridge or compressed air, into the animal's brain. Animals are considered to be properly stunned—that is, fully unconscious—when there is no attempt by the animal to stand up and right itself. After stunning, industry standards require that animals be stuck, which cuts off the blood supply to the brain, and then bled; it is the bleeding that finally causes death. At this point, animals are sent down the production line to be processed for their meat.

1. Humane Methods of Livestock Slaughter Act, 7 U.S.C.A. § 1902.

Despite these requirements for humane slaughter, federal inspectors often have had very little enforcement authority and animals reportedly are routinely mistreated. Investigations have revealed animals being kicked, beaten, and abused during transport and while being handled at slaughterhouses, and advocates claim that many are often ineffectively stunned, so that they are still alive and conscious when they are processed.

In fact, a 2001 article in the *The Washington Post* titled "They Die Piece by Piece" described a grisly reality inside slaughterhouses in which animals reached processing stations and were cut, skinned, or scalded while they were still clearly conscious. The article claimed that slaughterhouse workers are pressured to work so quickly that they cannot make sure every animal is properly stunned. Federal inspectors try to catch violations, but they complained to *Post* reporters that their authority has been reduced and that they typically do not have access to parts of the plant where animals are killed. According to the *Post*, part of the problem was that government policies had relaxed oversight and given more responsibility to the industry to self-monitor. The article noted, for example, that the government failed to take action against a Texas beef company despite the fact that the company was cited twenty-two times in 1998 for serious violations that included chopping hooves off live cattle.

Moreover, animal advocates point out that the HMLSA completely fails to cover poultry and fish, two of the most popular food animals, as well as other small animals, like rabbits, that are also slaughtered for food. As a result, animal rights advocates say that billions of chickens, turkeys, and ducks are processed while still alive. The process calls for chickens to be shackled upside down on a production line, immobilized by an electrified water bath, passed through a machine that is supposed to slice their necks, and then dropped into scalding water to loosen their feathers, but activists say that the fast pace of the production line results in many chickens that are not properly immobilized or beheaded, and that end up being scalded to death.

There are reasons to believe that the welfare of farm animals can be improved, however. Since *The Washington Post* exposé, Congress has substantially increased the amount of funding allocated for enforcement of the HMLSA. This has allowed the USDA to hire more inspectors and implement better systems to uncover and track violations of the humane slaughter law. In addition, a new cost-effective procedure for the humane killing of birds—Controlled-Atmosphere Killing, a system that uses gas—may soon help improve the plight of chicken and other birds, allowing them to be humanely killed while still in their transport crates rather than roughly mishandled by workers on the production line. Slaughter is never pleasant, but animal advocates hope to ensure that it is done with minimal distress to the animals.

The issue of animal welfare is perhaps the most controversial area of the factory farm debate. Animal rights advocates seek to improve not only the way that animals are slaughtered but also the way that they are treated throughout their short lives. Industry representatives, on the other hand, point to improvements in animal welfare standards and animal care, and see production and low meat prices as the priority goals. The viewpoints in this chapter represent some of the differing points of view about this important issue.

Producers of Animal Food Products Are Committed to Animal Welfare

Animal Agriculture Alliance

The Animal Agriculture Alliance is a group of individuals, companies, and organizations whose mission is to promote the benefits of animal agriculture.

Farmers, ranchers and veterinarians have an ethical obligation to care for animals raised for food. It is their duty to ensure the safety, health and overall well-being of the animals. The well-being of the animal is critical to providing quality food products for their families, employees and all consumers.

Training each animal caretaker is of the utmost importance to ensuring the best animal care possible. This is why farms participate in certification programs, distance-learning courses and other means for continuing education on animal care.

Industry Commitments to Animal Welfare

Each segment of the livestock and poultry industries has species-specific educational programs, guidelines and best management practices focused on proper care, handling, facilities and transportation of animals. These programs and guidelines continue to evolve and improve as each industry gains a better understanding of what is necessary for the well-being of animals, through research.

Animal production facilities are built to maintain the health and safety of each animal. In many/most of today's production systems, animals are raised comfortably indoors;

this arrangement allows producers and veterinarians to closely monitor herd health, control temperature, ensure a nutritionally balanced diet and keep the animals safe from predators. Whether a large or small farm, providing the best care for animals is the highest priority; size is not a differentiator for how animals are treated.

The Humane Slaughter Act regulates the U.S. meat packing industry. Federal inspectors utilize the Act to ensure compliance in livestock packing plants on a frequent basis, and if violations are found, immediate action is taken. The livestock industry has voluntary guidelines in addition to the Act that meet even higher standards for animal care.

Standards for animal care should be based on the expertise of veterinarians, farmers, ranchers and animal scientists— the people who work with farm animals daily. American farmers and ranchers have been working with veterinarians, animal scientists, agricultural engineers and animal well-being experts to develop and support ethically grounded, science-based guidelines and audits.

Changes to animal well-being guidelines should be based on data, expert analysis and economic feasibility. Adding unnecessary costs to U.S. production will increase the amount of food imported from places that have an inferior record on food safety and animal well-being. Overzealous standards will increase the price of food, impacting all families trying to make ends meet.

Standards for animal care should be based on the expertise of veterinarians, farmers, ranchers and animal scientists—the people who work with farm animals daily.

Today, the marketplace offers meat, milk and eggs produced in a variety of systems. Consumers have the choice of buying protein from any system that meets their individual needs.

Because each livestock and poultry sector is committed to providing the best care for its food animals, each species has developed an animal welfare program to meet those best management practices.

Chickens

The physical well-being of animals is very important to the broiler chicken industry, especially since only healthy animals can be utilized for human food. To assist companies in ensuring and verifying a high level of welfare exists among their animals, the National Chicken Council developed the *NCC Animal Welfare Guidelines and Audit Checklist*, which has been widely adopted within the industry. It covers every phase of the chicken's life and offers science-based recommendations for proper treatment. Among other things, it includes chapters on:

- Education, training and planning

- Best practices on the farm

- Appropriate comfort and shelter

- Proper nutrition and feeding

- Catching and transportation

- Health care

- Processing

The physical well-being of animals is very important to the broiler chicken industry, especially since only healthy animals can be utilized for human food.

It is backed up by a detailed audit checklist that can be completed by the company itself, by a customer representative, or a third-party auditor. The NCC program was accepted in 2005 by the Food Marketing Institute and National Council of Chain Restaurants. . . .

Layer Hens (Eggs)

In 2002, the United Egg Producers (UEP) adopted guidelines for animal welfare developed by an independent third party Scientific Advisory Committee. Animal Husbandry Guidelines for Egg Laying Flocks provides science-based guidelines for all aspects of egg production, including the following:

- Cage configuration

- Handling

- Beak trimming

- Transportation and slaughter

- Cage space per bird

- Molting

- Cage free guidelines

These recommendations also became the basis for an animal-welfare certification initiative sponsored by UEP called "UEP Certified." The animal husbandry guidelines within the UEP Certified program are endorsed by the Food Marketing Institute and the National Council of Chain Restaurants and have been used as a model for the creation of animal husbandry guidelines by the International Egg Commission. In addition, UEP partners with the American Humane Association in the "American Humane Certified" program. This program establishes guidelines for egg production from hens in cage-free and free-range farm systems, thus it is a good balance to the UEP Certified program's certification of both modern cage housing and cage-free production systems.

Egg farmers who implement the UEP Certified program must be audited annually by USDA's Agricultural Marketing

Service or Validus [a private company that provides auditing services to the agricultural industry], to achieve and maintain their UEP Certified status. As well, producers must implement the guidelines in 100% of their production facilities regardless of where or how eggs are marketed. Today, more than 80% of all eggs in the United States are produced under the UEP Certified program. UEP has certified well-being programs for eggs raised in caged and cage-free systems. Consumers can now choose eggs from either and know that UEP Certified eggs come from a scientifically validated, independently audited well-being program. . . .

Ducks

The U.S. Duck Council is committed to promoting and maintaining comprehensive animal welfare standards throughout the White Pekin duckling industry. The U.S. Duck Council and its members produce quality food products for consumers, while ensuring that ducks receive humane treatment. Ducks are raised according to the highest standards, by upholding scientifically based animal husbandry practices. The U.S. Duck Council's animal welfare standards were developed in conjunction with animal husbandry experts. Elements of the standards include:

- Health and hygiene
- Shelter and growing environment
- Biosecurity
- Transportation and handling

Turkeys

The turkey industry has long held that appropriate treatment of turkeys is a necessary part of production and the *National Turkey Federation (NTF) Humane Production Guidelines* have been in place in the industry since the late 1980s. The most recent guidelines identify control points in turkey production and processing, and provide recommendations to ensure animal welfare standards in the following areas:

- Farm safety and security

- Hatching

- Facilities and equipment

- Feed and water supply

- Maintenance

- Bird comfort

- Training

These guidelines represent the most up-to-date scientific information available to ensure the health and well-being of turkeys, and they continue to be updated as new scientific data, technologies and/or processes become available. Developed by leading turkey industry experts, the guidelines have been evaluated and approved through numerous third-party scientific reviews. Third-party scientific reviews by the Federation of Animal Science Societies' (FASS) Animal Welfare Committee and the American Association of Avian Pathologists' (AAAP) Welfare Subcommittee as well as the AAAP Board of Directors, received approval and support. Both organizations praised the *NTF Animal Care Guidelines* as a well-written document and a model program for the turkey industry to follow. . . .

Swine

The National Pork Board supports animal welfare guidelines based on sound science through the Pork Quality Assurance Plus™ program. PQA Plus™ was created to integrate industry practices that insure food safety and animal welfare; it was developed by several university researchers, pork producers representing 13 states and all production system types and allied industry representatives. The program combines guidelines for providing proper care to improve swine well-being with curriculum that specifically addresses caretaker training, animal observation, emergency back-up support, space allocation, timely euthanasia, facilities, handling and movement, ventilation and air quality, and zero tolerance for willful acts of abuse. Most major packers require producers to be PQA Plus certified to ensure the food animals meet quality assurance protocols. The program has three stages, as follows:

- Individual certification through producer education

- Site status through on-farm site assessment

- Opportunity for on-farm audits

PQA Plus™ demonstrates the commitment U.S. pork producers make to providing pork that is safe, high quality and responsibly produced. . . .

The industry also administers a Transport Quality Assurance (TQA) program. It provides guidelines on handling, loading, transport, and unloading of all sizes of pigs. The program is geared toward on-farm animal handlers, transporters, and those who handle pigs at the destination site. It is a voluntary education/certification program that may be required by packers and producers.

Dairy Cattle

The National Milk Producers Federation, in conjunction with the Milk and Beef Dairy Quality Assurance (DQA) Center, introduced the *Caring for Dairy Animals Technical Reference Guide and On-The-Dairy Self-Evaluation Guide* in 2002 to serve as a reference manual for dairy producers. The manual addresses all key elements of dairy animal care and recommends best management practices. Some areas of focus in the manual are:

- Producer and employee training

- Dairy nutritional care: watering and feeding

- Transporting and handling animals

- Birth and management of calves

Also included in the *Guide* is a voluntary self-audit checklist for producers. The self-audit addresses quality control points that can be objectively observed by the producer and help the producer enhance their existing animal care practices. These dairy animal care guidelines are endorsed by the National Council of Chain Restaurants (NCCR) and the Food Marketing Institute (FMI)....

Because the dairy industry has various sectors, it created a National Dairy Animal Well-Being Initiative, a producer-led coalition that includes each sector of the industry, which is proposing a set of principles and guidelines intended to provide a uniform umbrella of assurance that the industry is meeting its ethical obligation for dairy animal well-being. The goal is to demonstrate dairy producers' commitment to animal well-being.

Veal Calves

The American veal industry has committed to a complete transition to group housing by 2017, a move that underscores the industry's commitment to the health and well-being of its animals. Presently, over 10 percent of veal is reared in group housing, and the current industry Veal Quality Assurance Program standards require animal welfare be certified by an attending veterinarian.

The American Veal Association is calling for continued research and investment in animal husbandry and group production technology, so an integrated welfare model that combines environment, facility design, health, handling and behavior is available to all producers....

Beef Cattle

The Beef Quality Assurance (BQA) program provides a producer-driven approach to producing the safest and best quality beef possible. The program began in 1987 and is supported by the National Cattlemen's Beef Association (NCBA), an organization funded by beef producers nationwide and the Beef Checkoff. The BQA program provides guidelines for livestock care and handling, nutrition and veterinary treatment. Cattlemen can become BQA certified when they meet criteria for quality beef production set forth in the BQA guidelines. Producers also undergo continuous training to remain certified. Most states have individual BQA programs and can offer their own certification standards. State certification requirements vary, but may include third party verification and testing procedures to ensure good management practices. . . .

Quality assurance during transportation also plays a critical role in the health and welfare of beef cattle, as proper handling and transport of cattle can reduce sickness in calves, prevent bruises, and improve the quality of the meat from these animals. The NCBA Master Cattle Transporter program (for cattle transporters) is part of the BQA initiative. The program consists of educational materials in a manual and on a training video. The Master Cattle Transporter Guide educates on properly moving cattle up to and in to the trailer, distributing cattle correctly on the trailer, hauling techniques that reduce cattle stress and handling emergency situations. A transportation quality assurance for stocker trailers is currently being developed. The Master Cattle Transporter program was developed utilizing the expertise of animal handling and transport consultants, producers, auction operators, feed yard managers, packer representatives and University researchers/experts. . . .

In addition to NCBA programs and state BQA programs, other organizations offer quality assurance programs, such as the certification provided by the Texas Cattle Feeders Association (TCFA). The TCFA program includes a third-party review and annual audit by a veterinarian or nutritionist to ensure criteria are met for nutrition, disease prevention, identification, and adequate shelter and housing.

Sheep

The *Sheep Care Guide*, sponsored by the American Sheep Industry Association (ASI), provides sheep producers with research-based guidelines in such areas as nutrition, facilities and handling, animal health, transportation and managing predation to assist them in providing optimum care for their sheep. Originally published in 1996, the 2005 edition has been updated and expanded to include relevant new research findings regarding animal care. ASI's well-known publication, the *Sheep Production Handbook*, provides producers a resource of in-depth background information for designing and implementing their specific farm management plans and is frequently used as a classroom textbook at colleges and universities. The ASI Sheep Safety and Quality Assurance Program provides producer-level training and certification in total quality management including proper handling and care of sheep. . . .

In 1991, the [U.S. meat packing] industry teamed with leading animal welfare expert Dr. Temple Grandin to develop voluntary guidelines that took federal regulations a step further.

Packing/Processing

The U.S. meat packing industry for livestock is regulated by the Humane Slaughter Act. Federal inspectors in plants during every minute of operation ensure compliance with this important law and can take immediate action for violations.

In 1991, the industry teamed with leading animal welfare expert Dr. Temple Grandin to develop voluntary guidelines that took federal regulations a step further. In 1997, the American Meat Institute and Dr. Grandin developed an audit program to measure key factors in plants that can indicate stress, like how often livestock vocalize, whether they slip or fall, and how often they must be prodded to encourage them to walk forward. By measuring welfare using objective criteria, the industry improved welfare in plants dramatically. Today, this audit program has become a global animal welfare standard. Compliance with the standard is often required in order to sell meat to key customers.

The Meat Packing Industry Promotes the Welfare of Animals

American Meat Institute

The American Meat Institute is a national trade association that represents companies that process 95 percent of red meat and 70 percent of turkey in the United States and their suppliers throughout America.

Many religious laws from different faiths have formed the basis for modern livestock processing practices. One common theme among all faiths has been a respect for animals, avoidance of animal suffering and appreciation for the nourishment that they provide. These themes permeate the practices of the meat packing industry.

In 1958, Congress passed the Humane Slaughter Act, which laid out specific rules for livestock treatment in meat plants that sold meat products to the federal government. In 1978, the law was reauthorized and expanded to cover all federally inspected meat plants (except those performing religious slaughter). But beginning in the early 1990s, the meat industry embarked on a proactive effort to enhance animal welfare in meat plants.

Working with leading experts, including Dr. Temple Grandin, associate professor of animal science at Colorado State University, the industry began to embrace the idea that enhanced welfare had distinct additional benefits, including:

- *Enhanced meat quality*. Calm animals produce better meat products with fewer quality defects.

- *Enhanced plant efficiency.* Animals that are calm and humanely handled move easily through processing plants.

- *Improved worker safety.* Calm livestock reduce the chance that an employee will become injured by an animal.

- *Enhanced morale.* When animals are handled humanely, employees tend to have better attitudes toward their jobs.

Government Oversight

The U.S. meat industry is one of the most heavily regulated industries in the nation. Thousands of pages of regulations govern every aspect of the meat packing business, including how livestock are treated. The Humane Slaughter Act of 1978 dictates strict animal handling and slaughtering practices for packing plants. Those standards are monitored by Food Safety and Inspection Service (FSIS) inspectors nationwide, who are present in packing plants during every minute of operation. FSIS inspectors are empowered to take action in a plant any time they identify a violation of the Act.

Humane slaughter rules require:

- That animals must be handled and moved through chutes and pens in ways that do not cause stress.

- That livestock must be rendered insensible to pain prior to slaughter. The Act details the methods that must be used to stun animals.

- That animals must have access to water and that those kept longer than 24 hours must have access to feed.

- That animals kept in pens overnight must be permitted plenty of room to lie down.

- That non-ambulatory livestock in the stockyards, crowd pens or stunning chutes may not be dragged.

These federal requirements are the minimum standards for animal welfare. Industry's own voluntary standards take federal requirements a step further.

Voluntary Efforts and Audits

In 1991, the industry asked Dr. Temple Grandin to author the landmark *Recommended Animal Handling Guidelines for Meat Packers.* Five years later, Dr. Grandin completed an audit of meat packing plants for the U.S. Department of Agriculture and concluded that animal welfare evaluations need not be subjective. Rather, she said they could be measured using numeric criteria.

In addition to a natural, human concern for animals, there are distinct economics benefits that result from humane handling.

In 1997, AMI [American Meat Institute] asked Dr. Grandin to develop a new audit tool using objective criteria that could be used by plants to monitor their own animal welfare practices. She developed *Good Management Practices for Animal Handling and Stunning* and the "AMI audit" was born. This audit program was embraced first by leading quick service restaurant chains and later by major retailers.

As part of the audits, plants measure criteria that include:

- Livestock vocalizations that may indicate stress

- Slips and falls that can cause injury

- The accuracy of stunning

- The effectiveness of stunning techniques in animals that are insensitive to pain.

- The use of electric prods

By measuring and monitoring these criteria over time, plants can determine when variations occur and can correct problems promptly.

. As part of AMI's proactive efforts, the Institute in 1997 launched the Animal Care & Handling Conference, now an annual conference held in February in Kansas City. In 2007, nearly 300 people attended the conference.

In 2002, the American Meat Institute Board of Directors took another proactive step by voting to make animal welfare a non-competitive issue among the Institute's members. Today, members share information that can enhance welfare and welcome each other into plants in an effort to share best practices.

In 2005, AMI merged the 1991 and 1997 documents in the comprehensive 2005 Animal Handling and Audit Guide. The guide, which was updated again in 2007, includes standardized audit forms. . . .

Economic Benefits of Humane Handling

In addition to a natural, human concern for animals, there are distinct economics benefits that result from humane handling.

When an animal is stressed due to heat, anxiety, rough treatment or environmental factors, the meat that comes from the animal will be of a lesser quality. For example, if an animal becomes agitated in the chute, stress hormones like adrenalin are released, and muscle pH drops. In cattle, this can result in "dark cutters," or dark spots, in meat. In hogs, this can cause Pale Soft Exudative (PSE) tissue, which appears as pale, soft spots in pork. These quality defects cause direct economic losses to meat companies.

Numerous studies have been done that detail the financial losses that can be attributed to these stress-related quality defects.

In order to maintain optimal efficiency, meat plants depend on a continuous supply of livestock moving through the plants. Animals that are calm and well-handled typically will move through the chutes more easily, which enables the process to operate efficiently.

Data Reflect Improvement

Data collected by Grandin through surveys done annually since 1996 demonstrated consistent, sustained improvement in livestock handling and stunning. . . .

In addition, a 2001 survey of American Meat Institute members reflects an increasing focus on animal handling and stunning by meat plants. According to the results, 93 percent of beef plants and 92 percent of pork plants conduct animal handling and stunning self-audits. Twenty-three percent of auditing beef plants and 32 percent of auditing pork plants said their audits had resulted in strong improvements in handling/stunning. Seventy percent of auditing beef plants and 73 percent of auditing pork plants report modest improvements in animal handling and stunning.

Optimal welfare clearly is good for livestock—and for business.

Seventy-nine percent of beef plants and 81 percent of pork plants indicated that they had hired a consultant to resolve animal handling and stunning problems. Ninety-three percent of beef plants and 81 percent of pork plants said they had purchased special equipment like a restrainer to improve handling and/or stunning.

The Future

The U.S. meat industry is committed to finding new ways to enhance animal handling and stunning in plants even further.

Many academic papers and presentations have been given on this subject. Each year summary presentations are deliv-

ered at the AMI Foundation Animal Care and Handling Conference for the food industry. . . .

The U.S. meat packing industry will seek new ways to
continually improve animal welfare in the meat industry by
monitoring research, sharing best practices and embracing
training programs. Optimal welfare clearly is good for livestock—and for business.

Providing Humans with Quality Food Is More Important than Animal Welfare

Justine Brian

Justine Brian is the national administrator of the United Kingdom's schools debating competition, Debating Matters.

Before the Second World War chicken was a relatively expensive meat, with the UK [United Kingdom] population eating less than a kilo per annum [year]—compared to today's average of 23kg per person. After the war, as part of the government's concerted efforts to ensure the UK was self-sufficient in food and able to move away from postwar rationing (which lasted almost a decade after the war ended), the industrial-scale production of chicken began. Today, 93 per cent of the fresh chicken we purchase, most of it produced in the UK, is reared on factory farms.

Opposition to Factory Farming

The issue of how we produce chicken made the front page of last Friday's [January 4, 2008] *Independent* [a British newspaper] thanks to a new series of shows on Channel 4. This week, the channel launched a season of campaigning programmes called 'The Big Food Fight', starring the channel's three superstar celebrity chefs: restaurateur and king of on-screen swearing, Gordon Ramsay; trendy lifestyle chef turned saviour of school meals, Jamie Oliver; and Eton-educated smallholder and killer of squirrels, bunnies and anything else that might make a good dinner, Hugh Fearnley-Whittingstall.

In the first strand of this campaigning season, *Hugh's Chicken Run*, Fearnley-Whittingstall launches his 'Chicken

Out' campaign to persuade UK supermarkets to only stock free-range chicken, and to persuade us, the consumers, to stop buying factory-farmed birds. Fearnley-Whittingstall is hardly a friend of vegetarians; his previous exploits in his *River Cottage* programmes have enraged animal rights campaigners and the squeamish alike. Yet, in *Chicken Run*, his argument is that factory-farmed chickens suffer whereas free-range ones are happier because of the conditions in which they are kept; he has no problem with eating meat as long as the animals concerned live a 'natural' life.

Unsurprisingly blanked by the factory chicken farmers of the UK when he asks to visit their farms to demonstrate how cruel they are to their livestock, the *River Cottage* star decides to set up his own small-scale factory chicken farm, alongside a free-range farm for comparison, with both enterprises run to standard UK farming guidelines.

The other side to his campaign is to persuade a group of people who would ordinarily buy the factory-farmed two-chickens-for-a-fiver at their local supermarket to try free-range meat. Because so many people have opposed his arguments by pleading poverty, he persuades a group of people from a run-down local housing estate in his home town of Axminster, south-west England, to rear their own animals on a section of nearby allotments. A group of a dozen-or-so locals go along with the plan, though they seem initially more impressed with the fact that they are talking to their neighbours than with the business of farming. It may not be a practical way of feeding themselves, but you can bet the government's social inclusion advisers were applauding every moment.

Along the way, Fearnley-Whittingstall cooks some really nice food to prove that free-range chicks are best (though a chef-prepared risotto would surely taste good regardless of where the chicken came from); persuades a local tool company's canteen to 'do a Jamie Oliver', that is, dump catering cuisine and cook 'real' food instead; and finally, as is common to most TV production today, he makes some Axminster locals cry about their lifestyle choices (with weeping children for extra moral pressure!) when they visit his factory-farmed bird shed.

> There is no reason to know who farmed my chicken or how, as long as it is produced to some decent, minimum standard with human welfare paramount.

Happily, one of the Axminster locals, a generously proportioned single mum called Hayley, rather impressively refuses to cry or get upset on cue for the cameras. The reality of chicken farming is exactly what she imagined it might be like, she says. She'd probably prefer to eat the free-range stuff, but she's just fine with intensive farming as it means she can afford to eat chicken and feed her family. She clearly hadn't read the script.

Bogus Animal Welfare Arguments

I suspect most people would be surprised, perhaps even shocked, about what commercial livestock farming looks like and that's because, thankfully, most of us no longer have to produce our own food, and are far removed from the meat products we buy at the supermarket. And why shouldn't we be? One of the many benefits of the Industrial Revolution was a division of labour in society—and in this instance, that means that someone else produces my food and distributes it to a central purchasing point near my home, while I do some other job I specialise in. There is no reason to know who farmed my chicken or how, as long as it is produced to some decent, minimum standard with *human* welfare paramount.

An equivalent of the foodie obsession with the provenance of our food might be for me to demand to visit the Polish mine where the coal that lights and heats my home is extracted so I understand the source of this fuel and how it's produced. If I was a real trainspotter, I'd also want to know the name of the individual Polish miner who personally dug the coal for me. As it happens, the coal analogy makes more sense than Fearnley-Whittingstall's campaign; I *do* give a damn about the people who undertake the relatively dangerous task of mining as they are my fellow human beings; I really don't give a stuff about a broiler chicken.

Fearnley-Whittingstall's premise for his campaign is laid out clearly at the start of the first programme when he says: 'To me, it shouldn't be possible to produce a chicken for £2.50' [€2.50 or about $3.50]. This is because he thinks that chickens should be produced in a more labour-intensive way (free-range birds grow slower, are housed in lower densities and so take more human input to produce an eating bird). In Fearnley-Whittingstall's world, the price of the average chicken would be at least double what we currently pay for a super-market Grade A chicken. Presumably, a takeaway from KFC and a Marks and Spencer [a large department store in Britain] chicken sandwich would become more expensive, too. Why would we want to make our food more expensive?

While humans may find conditions in a broiler shed crowded and boring, that doesn't mean that those animals are suffering in any way.

As it happens, the animal welfare argument is somewhat bogus. What is good for a human being is not necessarily what is good for an animal. While animal welfare activists complain about the cramming of chickens into sheds, the programme makes clear that the free-range chickens are also at risk from health problems. The intensively produced chickens are bred to bulk up quickly and sometimes suffer leg problems as a result. The free-range birds, exposed to the outside world, are at greater risk of disease. Good stock management means that the relatively small proportion of chickens that do not thrive in either system, due to disease, injury or congential problems, are swiftly culled.

Even if farmers were heartless bastards who were careless about animal suffering (which they generally are not), they have a strong economic incentive not to carry on feeding chickens that won't make the grade at the end of the 40–50 days required to fatten them up. While humans may find conditions in a broiler shed crowded and boring, that doesn't mean that those animals are suffering in any way.

Humans Before Chickens

Chickens are food, and producing food efficiently is not 'unethical'. If we put animal welfare before human convenience across the range of meat products that we consume, as the likes of Fearnley-Whittingstall believe we should, the result would be that for many people meat would be a rare treat that they could only eat perhaps once or twice a week. Of course, that restriction wouldn't apply to the kind of well-off person who laps up the crusades of celebrity chefs, frets about their food labels and already pays over-the-odds for 'ethical' posh nosh.

It's a good thing that people need to spend less of their income on simply sustaining themselves. If we have to spend less on the basics of survival then we've more money to spend on a whole world of other things. We may even choose to blow some extra cash on a free-range chicken from time to time, but it's better that we can choose if and when we do that rather than having this foisted upon us by others who believe animal welfare is more important than having a bit more cash in our pockets.

The views put forward in 'The Big Food Fight' season are increasingly common ones espoused by an evangelical fooderati. This isn't about chickens at all. It's about a disgust at large-scale food production, our unhindered consumerism, our uneducated palates, all-powerful supermarkets, and our supposedly gross overconsumption. Packing a third less chickens in a factory shed and giving them rubber balls to play with, as illustrated in *Hugh's Chicken Run*, is about making us feel a little bit better about eating them. The discussion about what's 'natural' for chickens also helps to maintain a Disney-fied image of what farming looks like—something that looks rather like the *River Cottage* world we've watched over the past few years. As Fearnley-Whittingstall says in this new show, 'this isn't farming as I know it'. But *River Cottage* shows farming for the privileged few; it's not the way you feed a nation of 60 million people.

For me, it's no contest. When it comes down to providing good cheap protein for human consumption over the welfare of a 39-day-old chicken, the human wins every time.

The Treatment of Animals in Factory Farms Is a Serious Moral Wrong

Peter Singer

Peter Singer is a philosopher and professor of bioethics at Princeton University, laureate professor at the University of Melbourne, and a well-known animal rights advocate.

There is a growing consensus that factory farming of animals—also known as CAFOs, or concentrated animal feeding operations—is morally wrong. The American animal rights movement, which in its early years focused largely on the use of animals in research, now has come to see that factory farming represents by far the greater abuse of animals. The numbers speak for themselves. In the United States somewhere between 20 million and 40 million birds and mammals are killed for research every year. That might seem like a lot—and it far exceeds the number of animals killed for their fur, let alone the relatively tiny number used in circuses—but 40 million represents less than two days' toll in America's slaughterhouses, which kill about 10 billion animals each year.

Lives of Suffering

The overwhelming majority of these animals have spent their entire lives confined inside sheds, never going outdoors for a single hour. Their suffering isn't just for a few hours or days, but for all their lives. Sows and veal calves are confined in crates too narrow for them even to turn around, let alone walk a few steps. Egg-laying hens are unable to stretch their wings because their cages are too small and too crowded. With nothing to do all day, they become frustrated and attack each other. To prevent losses, producers sear off their beaks with a hot knife, cutting through sensitive nerves.

Chickens, reared in sheds that hold 20,000 birds, now are bred to grow so fast that most of them develop leg problems because their immature bones cannot bear the weight of their bodies. Professor John Webster of the University of Bristol's School of Veterinary Science said: "Broilers are the only livestock that are in chronic pain for the last 20 percent of their lives. They don't move around, not because they are overstocked, but because it hurts their joints so much."

Sometimes their legs collapse under them, causing them to starve to death because they cannot reach their food. Of course, the producers then cannot sell these birds, but economically, they are still better off with the freakishly fastgrowing breeds they use. As an article in an industry journal noted, "simple calculations" lead to the conclusion that often "it is better to get the weight and ignore the mortality." Another consequence of the genetics of these birds is that the breeding birds—the parents of the ones sold in supermarkets—constantly are hungry, because, unlike their offspring that are slaughtered at just 45 days old, they have to live long enough to reach sexual maturity. If fed as much as they are programmed to eat, they soon would be grotesquely obese and die or be unable to mate. So they are kept on strict rations that leave them always looking in vain for food.

Human Dominion over Animals Requires Mercy

Opposition to factory farming, once associated mostly with animal rights activists, now is shared by many conservatives, among them Matthew Scully, a former speech writer in President George W. Bush's White House and the author of *Dominion: The Power of Man, the Suffering of Animals, and the Call to Mercy*. In Scully's view, even though God has given us "dominion" over the animals, we should exercise that dominion with mercy—and factory farming fails to do so. Scully's writings have found support from other conservatives, like Pat Buchanan, editor of *The American Conservative*, which gave cover-story prominence to Scully's essay "Fear Factories: The Case for Compassionate Conservatism—for Animals," and George F. Will, who used his *Newsweek* column to recommend Scully's book.

No less a religious authority than Pope Benedict XVI has stated that human "dominion" over animals does not justify factory farming. While head of the Roman Catholic Church's Sacred Congregation for the Doctrine of the Faith, the future pope condemned the "industrial use of creatures, so that geese are fed in such a way as to produce as large a liver as possible, or hens live so packed together that they become just caricatures of birds." This "degrading of living creatures to a commodity" seemed to him "to contradict the relationship of mutuality that comes across in the Bible."

No Redeeming Features

Some people think that factory farming is necessary to feed the growing population of our planet. The truth, however, is the opposite. No matter how efficient intensive pork, beef, chicken, egg and milk production becomes, in the narrow sense of producing more meat, eggs or milk for each pound of grain we feed the animals, raising animals on grain remains wasteful. Far from increasing the total amount of food available for human consumption, it reduces it.

[Factory farming] has nothing going for it except that it produces food that is, at the point of sale, cheap. But for that low price, the animals . . . have to pay steeply.

A concentrated animal feeding operation is, as the name implies, an operation in which we concentrate the animals and feed them. Unlike cattle or sheep on pasture, they don't feed themselves. There lies the fundamental environmental flaw: Every CAFO relies on cropland, on which the food the animals eat is grown. Because the animals, even when confined, use much of the nutritional value of their food to move, keep warm and form bone and other inedible parts of their bodies, the entire operation is an inefficient way of feeding humans. It places greater demands on the environment in terms of land, energy and water than other forms of farming. It would be more efficient to use the cropland to grow food for humans to eat.

Factory farming, overwhelmingly dominated by huge corporations like Tyson, Smithfield, ConAgra and Seaboard, has contributed to rural depopulation and the decline of the family farm. It has nothing going for it except that it produces food that is, at the point of sale, cheap. But for that low price, the animals, the environment and rural neighborhoods have to pay steeply.

Fortunately there are alternatives, including eating a vegan diet, or buying animal products only from producers who allow their animals to go outside and live a minimally decent life. It is time for a shift in our values. While our society focuses on issues like gay marriage and the use of embryos for research, we are overlooking one of the big moral issues of our day. We should see the purchase and consumption of factory-farm products, whether by an individual or by an institution like a university, as a violation of the most basic ethical standards of how we should treat animals and the environment.

Standard Factory Farming Practices Constitute Legalized Animal Abuse

The Humane Society of the United States

The Humane Society of the United States is the largest animal protection organization in the nation and a leader in farm animal advocacy.

In just one hour in the United States, more than one million land animals are killed for food. Before their slaughter, most of these farm animals—nearly ten billion each year— endure lives of abuse with virtually no legal protection at all. Considering this staggering figure, the mistreatment of farm animals is among the gravest animal welfare problems in the nation. Instead of being recognized as the social, intelligent individuals they are, chickens, pigs, cows, turkeys, and other animals are treated as mere meat-, egg-, and milk-production units and denied expression of many natural behaviors. And six standard agribusiness practices are the most egregious of all.

Battery Cages

In the United States, approximately 95 percent of egg-laying hens are intensively confined in tiny, barren "battery cages"— wire enclosures stacked several tiers high, extending down long rows inside windowless warehouses. The cages offer less space per hen than the area of a single sheet of paper. Severely restricted inside the barren cages, the birds are unable to engage in nearly any of their natural habits, including nesting, perching, walking, dust bathing, foraging, or even spreading their wings.

While many countries are banning the abusive battery cage system, U.S. egg producers still overcrowd about 300 million hens in these cruel enclosures.

Fast Growth of Birds

More than nine out of ten land animals killed for human consumption in the United States are chickens raised for meat— called "broilers" by the industry. About nine billion of these birds are slaughtered every year. According to poultry welfare expert Ian Duncan, Ph.D., "Without a doubt, the biggest welfare problems for meat birds are those associated with fast growth." The chicken industry's selective breeding for fast-growing animals and use of growth-promoting antibiotics have produced birds whose bodies struggle to function and are on the verge of structural collapse. To put this growth rate into perspective, the University of Arkansas reports that if humans grew as fast as today's chickens, we'd weigh 349 pounds by our second birthday.

Consequently, 90 percent of chickens raised for meat have detectable leg problems and structural deformities, and more than 25 percent suffer from chronic pain as a result of bone disease.

More than 90 percent of female pigs, or sows, in the United States are kept in . . . individual metal stalls so small and narrow the animals can't even turn around.

Forced Feeding for Foie Gras

French for "fatty liver," the delicacy known as paté de foie gras is produced from the grossly enlarged liver of a duck or goose. Two to three times daily for several weeks, birds raised for foie gras are force-fed enormous quantities of food through a long pipe thrust down their throats into their stomachs. This deliberate overfeeding causes the birds' livers to swell as much as

10 times their normal size, seriously impairing liver function, expanding their abdomens, and making movements as simple as standing or walking difficult and painful. Several European countries have banned the force-feeding of birds for foie gras, and the state of California is phasing it out. The United Nations Food and Agriculture Organization (FAO) states that the "production of fatty liver for foie gras . . . raises serious animal welfare issues and it is not a practice that is condoned by FAO."

Gestation Crates and Veal Crates

During their four-month pregnancies, more than 90 percent of female pigs, or sows, in the United States are kept in desolate "gestation crates"—individual metal stalls so small and narrow the animals can't even turn around or move more than a step forward or backward. The state of Florida and the European Union (EU) have already begun phasing out the use of gestation crates because of their inherent cruelty, yet these inhumane enclosures are still the normal agribusiness practice of most U.S. pork producers.

Similarly, most calves raised for veal are confined in restrictive crates—generally chained by the neck—that also prohibit them from turning around. The frustration of natural behaviors takes an enormous mental and physical toll on the animals. As with gestation crates for pregnant pigs and battery cages for egg-laying hens, veal crates are widely known for their abusive nature and are being phased out in the EU but are still in use in the United States.

Long-Distance Transport

Billions of farm animals endure the rigors of transport each year in the United States, with millions of pigs, cows, and "spent" egg-laying hens traveling across the country. Overcrowded onto trucks that do not provide any protection from temperature extremes, animals travel long distances without food, water, or rest. The conditions are so stressful that in-transit death is considered common.

Federal regulations do not require that chickens, turkeys, and other birds be rendered insensible to pain before they are slaughtered.

Electric Stunning of Birds

At the slaughter plant, birds are moved off trucks, dumped from transport crates onto conveyors, and hung upside down by their legs in shackles. Their heads pass through electrified baths of water, intended to immobilize them before their throats are slit. From beginning to end, the entire process is filled with pain and suffering.

Federal regulations do not require that chickens, turkeys, and other birds be rendered insensible to pain before they are slaughtered. The shackling of the birds causes incredible pain in the animals, many of whom already suffer leg disorders or broken bones, and electric stunning has been found to be ineffective in consistently inducing unconsciousness.

As a result, fully conscious birds can—and do—miss the killing blade only to drown in the tanks of scalding water intended to loosen their feathers.

Factory Farms Violate the Christian Duty to Act as Stewards of God's Creation

Michael Bruner

Michael Bruner is a Presbyterian minister and an adjunct professor of religion at Azusa Pacific University in California.

"Man is what he eats." With these words, the great Russian Orthodox theologian Alexander Schmemann begins his seminal book "For the Life of the World," a meditation on what it means to live a sacramental life. These words might similarly serve as the overarching theme of The Humane Society of the United States' new All Creatures Great and Small campaign, which aims to raise awareness of our inherent responsibility as stewards of God's creation, and more specifically how that call to stewardship impacts the lives of animals.

The Abuse of Farm Animals

The first phase of this campaign focuses on farm animals, and egg-laying hens in particular. At any given moment in America, approximately 280 million hens are condemned to a life spent in battery cages, contraptions so tiny that the birds can never spread their wings. Ever. Their entire lives. And the factory farms that confine these hens don't think twice about the suffering they subject these animals to. In fact, they scarcely think of the hens as animals at all but treat them, instead, as nothing more than mere units of production whose eggs can be distributed.

The trouble, of course, is that these mere units of production are a part of God's handiwork, created with instincts to

Michael Bruner, "Faith and Factory Farms," *The Washington Post*, August 13, 2008. Reproduced by permission of the author.

spread their wings, walk around, nest, and live in cohesive social units. Hens are not widgets, in other words, but factory farms treat them as such.

If we humans can subject fellow creatures to such abhorrent conditions . . . what does this say about our inheritance as the only creatures made in the image of God?

The especially poignant element for Christians regarding the suffering of these animals is that Jesus, just before he himself was sent to slaughter, cries out in lament for his people, "Jerusalem, Jerusalem! . . . how many times I yearned to gather your children together, as a hen gathers her young under her wings. . . ." The master storyteller had countless metaphors at his disposal to explain his great love for his people, and he chooses the picture of a mother hen's love for her chicks. Contrast this beautiful picture of a protective love with the nightmare of today's factory farms and mother hens crammed together into battery cages and forced to lay eggs at unnaturally high rates, with never a chance to cover their young with her wings.

Religious Implications

This intolerable situation, along with the equally intolerable confinement of veal calves and pregnant sows in spaces so small they can never turn around, has fundamentally religious implications. If we humans can subject fellow creatures to such abhorrent conditions in order to merely satiate our appetites, what does this say about our inheritance as the only creatures made in the image of God? This is not solely an issue, in other words, of cruelty to animals, but of relinquishing our very identity as the imago dei ["image of god"].

The All Creatures Great and Small campaign addresses this imbalance in its very name: that is, all creatures great and small, humans and hens alike, deserve to be treated with compassion, not for mere sentimental reasons, but because we are all a part of God's good creation and should be treated with a commensurate respect and dignity.

The Humane Society of the United States seeks to honor our calling as stewards of God's creation by encouraging everyone to participate in one great month of compassion, where participants pledge either to switch to cage-free eggs or use egg substitutes for the month of October, beginning with the celebration of the feast of St. Francis, the patron saint of animals. While such a modest change won't solve all the problems associated with factory farming, it's certainly a worthwhile step that would help us take our obligation to be responsible stewards of creation more seriously.

CHAPTER 3

Does Factory Farming Harm Human Health or the Environment?

Chapter Preface

One of the most serious health concerns related to factory farming involves the widespread use of antibiotic drugs. Antibiotics have been used by industrial animal producers for many years—to prevent farm animals housed in crowded, often unhygenic conditions from getting sick, and to help them grow more quickly. According to a March 16, 2009 *New York Times* article by Nicholas D. Kristof, 70 percent of all antibiotics used in the United States are given to healthy livestock. Health experts and policymakers are becoming increasing alarmed by this practice, because the non-therapeutic overuse of antibiotics is contributing to the growth of dangerous, antibiotic-resistant pathogens that threaten human health. Many commentators, in fact, believe antibiotic resistance is reaching crisis proportions.

Antibiotic resistance occurs because, over time, infectious organisms such as bacteria evolve in ways that allow them to resist drugs that once would kill them. As a growing number of pathogens develop resistance to the arsenal of antibiotics traditionally used to treat them, and as fewer and fewer antibiotics are discovered and produced, humans are at risk of being infected by diseases that doctors thought they had conquered.

One of the most worrisome types of antibiotic-resistant infections, for example, is methicillin-resistant Staphylococcus aureus, or MRSA—a type of staph infection that is resistant to methicillin, an antibiotic. MRSA, often referred to in news reports as the "flesh-eating bacteria," is spreading rapidly, both in the United States and around the world. The MRSA infection often begins with a red spot on the skin that looks like a pimple, a boil, or a spider bite. In many cases, the body successfully fights the infection or minor skin infections occur that can be resolved with massive antibiotics. In rare instances, however, MRSA can attack parts of the body other than the skin and lead to life-threatening conditions, such as infections of the blood stream or heart valves, toxic shock syndrome, and pneumonia. In addition, MRSA is highly communicable, and infected people can easily transmit the infection to others. MRSA first emerged in hospitals, where it often spread easily among post-surgery and older, intensive-care patients, but today the MRSA threat is becoming increasingly common in community settings, such as schools and homes. According to some reports, MRSA now kills 18,000 people annually in the United States.

People can become infected with antibiotic-resistant bacteria from a variety of sources. Bacteria may be lurking on meat or other foods, and if not properly cooked, can be transferred to humans. Workers who have contact with farm animals at factory farms or who work in slaughterhouses also can act as carriers of resistant bacteria on their shoes or clothing. Similarly, wild animals who live in the vicinity of factory farms may transmit resistance bacteria to the wider community. Indeed, studies have found that residents living near factory farms where antibiotics are routinely given to farm animals are more likely to carry antibiotic-resistant bacteria.

Antibiotic-resistant bacteria can also be spread throughout the environment, affecting even people who live far away from factory farms. Antibiotics fed to animals enter the environment through animal wastes, and when these wastes enter the soil and groundwater, they can encourage bacteria in the larger environment to become antibiotic-resistant. In the United States, the amount of antibiotics excreted into the environment from animal wastes is massive—more than thirteen million pounds (or six million kilograms) annually.

The problem of antibiotic-resistance has become so serious that lawmakers are beginning to consider banning antibiotic use on factory farms. The European Union has already banned the use of antibiotics to promote the growth of livestock animals when those drugs also are used to treat people. The U.S. Centers for Disease Control and Prevention has urged the U.S. government to do likewise, but so far no such action has been taken. The United States has banned the farm use of one antibiotic—enrofloxacin—which has been blamed for causing increasing resistance to Ciprofloxacin, a very common and important antibiotic used in humans. In addition, in March 2009, legislation was introduced in both the U.S. House of Representatives and the Senate aimed at phasing out the use of other antibiotics on factory farms. The legislation, called the Preservation of Antibiotics for Medical Treatment Act (PAMTA), would prohibit the routine use of human medicines in livestock, except when needed to treat sick animals.

The viewpoints included in this chapter address the issue of antibiotic resistance as well as other ways that factory farming affects human health and the environment, and they discuss some possible future solutions.

Industrial Food Animal Production Is a Growing Public Health Threat

Pew Commission on Industrial Farm Animal Production

The Pew Commission on Industrial Farm Animal Production is a group of experts from various fields formed to conduct a comprehensive, fact-based, and balanced examination of key aspects of the U.S. farm animal industry.

One of the most serious unintended consequences of industrial food animal production (IFAP) is the growing public health threat of these types of facilities. In addition to the contribution of IFAP to the major threat of antimicrobial resistance, IFAP facilities can be harmful to workers, neighbors, and even those living far from the facilities through air and water pollution, and via the spread of disease. Workers in and neighbors of IFAP facilities experience high levels of respiratory problems, including asthma. In addition, workers can serve as a bridging population, transmitting animal-borne diseases to a wider population. A lack of appropriate treatment of enormous amounts of waste may result in contamination of nearby waters with harmful levels of nutrients and toxins, as well as bacteria, fungi, and viruses, all of which can affect the health of people both near and far from IFAP facilities.

Antibiotic Resistance

Antibiotics are one type of antimicrobial. Antimicrobials are substances that kill bacteria or suppress their multiplication or growth, and include antibiotics, some minerals, metals, and synthetic agents.

The use of antibiotics for growth promotion began with the poultry industry in the 1940s when it discovered that the use of tetracycline-fermentation byproducts resulted in improved growth. Since then, the practice of adding low levels of antibiotics and growth hormones to stimulate growth and improve production and performance parameters has been common among IFAP operations for all species. Because any use of antibiotics results in resistance, this widespread use of low-level antibiotics in animals, along with use in treating humans, contributes to the growing pool of antimicrobial resistance in the environment.

Reports on the amount of antibiotics used in animals range from 17.8 to 24.6 million pounds per year.

The threat from antimicrobial resistance became more apparent in the 1990s as the number of cases of drug-resistant infections increased in humans. A World Health Organization (WHO) Report on Infectious Diseases published in 2000 expressed alarm at the spread of multi-drug–resistant infectious disease agents, and pointed to food as a major source of antimicrobial-resistant bacteria. Since the discovery of the growth-promoting and disease-fighting capabilities of antibiotics, farmers, fish-farmers, and livestock producers have used antimicrobials. This ongoing and often low-level dosing for disease prevention and growth inevitably results in the development of resistance in bacteria in or near livestock because a selective pressure that does not kill fosters resistance.

While it is difficult to measure what percent of resistant infections in humans are caused by antimicrobial use in agriculture as opposed to other settings, it can be assumed that the wider the use of antimicrobials, the greater the chance for the development of resistance. Reports on the amount of antibiotics used in animals range from 17.8 to 24.6 million pounds per year. The Union of Concerned Scientists estimates that 70% of the antibiotics used in the United States annually are used in farm animals.

As the amount of antimicrobials present in the general environmental pool becomes greater, so too does the chance of resistance developing within many different bacterial populations. This is due, in part, to the way resistance is spread between capable bacteria. For example, many bacteria live in the human digestive tract or on human skin. These are not normally harmful (and are often helpful). However, these harmless bacteria may still be capable of passing resistance to other bacteria that *are* harmful, or could then *become* harmful.

Groundwater contamination . . . can extend throughout the aquifer, affecting drinking water supplies far from the source of contamination.

Feed formulation further influences risks because the feeds supplied to confined animal populations are significantly different from the foraged feeds traditionally available to poultry, swine, or cattle.

Health Risks

IFAP not only causes concerns about the health of the animals present, but the basic production model creates concerns with respect to human health, as well. Health risks are a function of exposure, with those engaged directly in livestock production typically having more frequent and more concentrated exposures to chemical or infectious agents, and others, such as those involved in support services, having lower rates of exposure. Health risks may extend far from the IFAP facility, however. Groundwater contamination, for example, can extend throughout the aquifer, affecting drinking water supplies far from the source of contamination. Infectious agents arising in IFAP facilities may be transmissible from person to person in a community setting and well beyond. An infectious agent that originates at an IFAP facility may persist through meat processing and contaminate a consumer meat product, resulting in a serious disease far from the IFAP facility.

Agricultural workers may serve as a bridging population between their communities and animal confinement facilities. Because it is categorized as an agricultural process, IFAP is largely exempt from state and federal industrial exposure monitoring, inspection, injury–disease reporting, and surveillance. Without monitoring, it is extremely difficult for public health officials to reduce the occupational health risk associated with IFAP.

The toxic gases and organic dusts associated with IFAP facilities have the potential to produce upper respiratory irritation in confinement facility workers. The emissions from confinement facilities, however, may affect communities proximate to those facilities, as well as populations far away from these operations. In particular, the elderly, those with compromised respiratory systems or chronic conditions that limit their mobility, and children are at most risk of asthma and other respiratory illnesses. Depression and other symptoms have also been attributed to emissions from such facilities.

Factory Farming Damages Land and Water

George Wuerthner

George Wuerthner is a writer, ecologist, photographer, and author of more than thirty published books.

The impact of factory farming upon the American land and native biodiversity is seldom discussed, but animal protein production has a significant impact upon the Nation's land and water. The direct environmental problems like air or water pollution associated with large factory farming operations may be clear, but less obvious are the environmental impacts associated with the agricultural production of feed crops and other consequences associated with large factory farming operations.

Huge Acreages of Feed Crops and Biodiversity Loss

According to the Animal Feed Manufactors Association, one third of the world's grains are fed directly to animals. In developed countries the percentage of grains fed directly to livestock rises to 60%, with 80% of the grains in the United States fed to livestock. Since the United States is the leading producer of beef cattle in the world, it is also the top animal feed producer in the world, with more than double the acreage in animal feed production than its closest rival China. This means the majority of cropland in the United States is not growing food for direct human consumption as many presume, but is used to grow forage crops for domestic livestock, including chickens, hogs, and cattle. In fact, in the

United States, domestic livestock consume 5 times as much grain as the entire American population.

It takes a huge amount of grain crops to support livestock production. For instance, to produce 1 kg [1 kilogram, or about 2.2 pounds] of beef requires 7 kg [15.4 pounds] of feed grain. Though chickens are more efficient at converting grain to meat, the ratio is still two to one with 2 kg [4.4 pounds] of grain required to produce 1 kg [2.2 pounds] of meat. According to Cornell University's David Pimentel, if the cropland currently used to grow grain fed to livestock were directed towards growing crops for human consumption, we could feed 800 million additional people or more likely provide a decent meal for those whose diet is inadequate.

In order to feed concentrated, confined animals, huge acreages of America's best farmland have been converted into monocultures of often genetically modified crops that stretch for miles. The major feed crops are corn, soybeans, and hay/alfalfa with smaller amounts of other grains like oats, barley and even wheat. For instance, 22% of all wheat grown in the US ultimately ends up as animal feed, rather than in food products like bread or cereal consumed directly by humans.

While it's difficult to determine how much of any crop is used to feed confined animal operations as opposed to diverse small farming operations, the total impact of animal agriculture of any kind is significant. Consider these statistics.

Globally, production of livestock feed uses a third of the Earth's arable land. In the United States farmland production is even more skewed towards animal feed. In 2008 American farmers, primarily in the Mid-west, planted 87 million acres to feeder corn. Part of that acreage figure was due to demand for corn created by ethanol, but the bulk of the corn acreage is used for animal feed. By comparison, farmers only planted an average of 234,000 acres across the entire country to fresh market sweet corn, the plant we consume directly for corn on the cob, and other food.

To give some comparison, Montana, the fourth largest state in the nation, is 93 million acres in size. So imagine nothing but corn stretching east and west across Montana's 550 miles and north and south by 300 miles. This is a huge area to be plowed up, and planted to an exotic grass crop that requires huge inputs of pesticides and fertilizer to sustain. Similarly the acreage devoted to soybeans is huge. According to the USDA [U.S. Department of Agriculture], some 74.5 million acres was planted to soybeans in 2008. And despite the popularity of tofu and other soy based food products, less than 2% of the soybean crop is used for production of food for direct human consumption—with most of the annual soybean crop going for animal feed.

Hay and/or alfalfa are yet another significant crop for confined livestock production, primarily dairy cows and beef cattle. In the United States, approximately 59 million acres are planted to hay/alfalfa annually. To put this in perspective, Oregon is 60 million acres in size.

Though slightly better than a row crop like corn or soybeans as wildlife habitat, hay/alfalfa fields still represent a net loss in native biodiversity and wildlife habitat. Hay/alfalfa replace native vegetation, and often require excessive amounts of fertilizers, and are cut frequently destroying even their temporal value as hiding and nesting cover for many wildlife species.

Taken together these three animal feed crops cover a minimum area over 200 million plus acres. To put these figures of animal feed cropland into perspective, the amount of land used to grow the top ten fresh vegetables in the US (asparagus, broccoli, carrots, cauliflower, celery, head lettuce, honeydew melons, onions, sweet corn, and tomatoes) occupies about a million acres.

If you fly over or drive across Iowa, Illinois, Ohio, Missouri, and other Mid-western states, you'll pass mile after mile of corn and/or soybean fields. Growing these crops has led to the near-extirpation of native plant communities like the tall grass prairie. Less than 4% of the native tall grass prairie remains and in some states like Iowa, which has less than 0.1% of its original tall grass prairie left, tall grass prairie is functionally extinct. Plus "clean" farming eliminates what little natural vegetation used to remain as woodlots, fenceline strips, wetlands, and other natural areas that in the past supported native species with the agricultural matrix.

Huge acreages of America's best farmland have been converted into monocultures of often genetically modified crops that stretch for miles.

Destruction of native plant communities has had serious impacts on native biodiversity. Agriculture, including livestock production as well as crop production combined, is the number one source for species endangerment in the country, and this number would be higher if you were to add in the species that are negatively impacted by exotic species, many of which increase due to habitat modification by agricultural production.

Damage to Water Resources

Agriculture is also the largest user of US water resources, with confined animal operations the largest per capita consumer of water. Grain fed beef production uses 100,000 gallons of water to produce every kg of food. By comparison, a similar kg of water-hungry rice uses only 2000 gallons of water, while potatoes require a mere 500 gallons. The primary mission of most western reservoirs is water storage for irrigated agriculture. Even in California which grows the bulk of the nation's vegetables and fruits, the largest consumers of irrigation water in the state by acreage is irrigated hay/alfalfa production.

Thus the environmental impacts associated with these dams and reservoirs, such as barriers to salmon migration, changes in water flows and flooding, are one indirect cost of factory farming operations. Add to this the direct dewatering of rivers for hay and other forage crop production [and] the loss of ground water supplies by pumping, particularly of the Ogalla aquifer. It's easy to see why some argue that livestock production is the leading cause of water degradation.

Agriculture also degrades water in other more direct ways. Livestock produce 130 times the waste of the entire human population of the United States, and unlike the human waste which tend to be treated in sewage plants, most animal waste winds up on the land or in the water. Not surprisingly, livestock production is the leading cause of non-point surface water pollution, accounting for 72% of the pollution in rivers and 56% of the pollution in lakes.

Agriculture production is also the number one source for groundwater contamination in the nation, with 49 states reporting high nitrates and 43 states reporting pesticide production attributed to agricultural practices.

Agricultural production is the largest source for soil erosion in the United States with current rates exceeding soil production rates by 17 times, with 90% of US croplands losing soils above sustainable rates. Since the majority of the nation's cropland is growing animal feed, the majority of soil erosion is a direct consequence of this production. Another indirect consequence of factory farming is the energy used to grow and transport feed. Animal protein production uses eight times the fossil fuel energy as growing vegetables or grass fed livestock. Beef production [is] particularly energy costly, requiring 54 times the fossil fuel equivalent of non-grain fed sources of protein.

Lest we forget, livestock are a significant contributor to global warming. The world's livestock produces 25% of the global greenhouse gases, with the waste lagoons of factory farms contributing another 5%. And according to a UN [United Nations] report, the global livestock sector generates more greenhouse gas emissions measured in CO_2 equivalent—18 percent—than transport.

Much, though not all, of these environmental impacts would be reduced or avoided altogether if factory farming and other kinds of confined animal production were eliminated. A shift to smaller, diverse farms, and a reduction, if not outright elimination of meat consumption, would both contribute to a huge reduction in environmental impacts of animal agriculture.

Factory Farming Is Unleashing New Diseases Like Swine Flu

Ben Macintyre

Ben Macintyre is a writer and columnist for The Times, *a British newspaper.*

I once worked on a chicken farm. Actually "farm" is far too gentle a word for the way these chickens were raised, and "factory" sounds too clinical. This was the seventh circle of chicken hell, a clucking, stinking, filthy production line with just one aim: to produce the maximum quantity of edible meat, as fast and as cheaply as possible, regardless of quality, cruelty or hygiene.

The creatures were raised in vast hangars, living on a diet of hormones, antibiotics and cheap grain, thousands crushed together in their own dirt under artificial light, growing from chick to slaughter size in a few grim weeks. (The most accelerated lifespan is now just 40 days.)

That was on a kibbutz farm [a collective farm in Israel] more than 20 years ago, in the midst of what we can now see as a revolution in livestock production, when science, economics and human appetite combined to forge intensive animal farming on an industrial and global scale.

Those mass-produced chickens were evidently ill. Air had to be pumped into the fetid shed to stop them suffocating. They still died at a pitiful rate, from heart attacks and stress, their bones often too weak to carry the weight of their artificially enlarged bodies. These were "wastage". The carcasses were kicked into a pile, and eventually removed by digger.

One did not need to be a scientist to know that something very sick was being produced in that shed.

Incubators of Disease

As swine flu spreads, and fear spreads faster, it is worth re-membering that this, and other animal-to-human viruses, are partly man-made, the outcome of our hunger for cheap meat, the result of treating animals as if they were mere raw mate-rial to be exploited in any way that increases output and prof-its.

There is a tendency to see a flu outbreak, like the plagues of old, as an unstoppable natural event, a scourge visited on Man from above. But there is nothing natural about this form of disease: indeed, it stems from an abuse of nature.

Vast modern pig farms, like the huge poultry plants across the globe, are ideal incubators of disease, and many scientists believe that viral mutation can be directly linked to intensive modern agricultural techniques. With enfeebled animals packed into confined spaces, pathogens spread easily, creating new and virulent strains that may be passed on to humans. When dense populations of factory-farmed animals exist alongside crowded human habitations, the potential for disas-ter is vastly greater.

The stress of such vile living conditions makes mass-produced animals more vulnerable to contagion, while the concentration on a few, high-yield breeds has led to genetic erosion and weakened immunity. We have created an environ-ment in which a mild virus can evolve rapidly into a much more pathogenic and contagious form.

Six years ago virologists warned that swine flu was on "an evolutionary fast track". A US Public Health report last year pointed to "substantial evidence of pathogen movement be-tween and among these industrial-scale operations". A year earlier the UN [United Nations] food agency predicted that the risk of disease transmission from animals to humans would grow with increasingly intensive animal production.

During the latest bout of avian flu, governments and the livestock industry were quick to blame wild birds and small-scale farms for spreading the disease. With hindsight, it appears that poultry in backyard flocks were markedly more resistant to a virus that has been traced directly to huge factory farms.

Food celebrities such as Jamie Oliver and Hugh Fearnley-Whittingstall have raised public awareness of the way modern meat is produced. But such campaigns tend to focus on the bland taste, ethical or environmental issues such as the toxic waste produced by factory farming, or the amount of water needed to produce a single kilo [1 kilogram, or about 2.2 pounds] of beef (16,000 litres [or about 4.23 thousand gallons]).

Mass-produced meat can kill you, even if you never eat it.

Far less attention has been paid to the more direct threat to public health posed by industrialised meat production, in which the basics of animal husbandry have been ignored. This, in turn, can be traced to the astonishing transformation in the world's meat-eating habits.

A Threat to World Health

Humanity is more carnivorous today then ever before, thanks to selective breeding techniques, low world grain prices, global distribution networks and the Chinese economic boom. In 1965 the Chinese ate just 4kg of meat per head per annum: today the average Chinese citizen consumes 54kg a year.

The number of animals on the planet has increased by nearly 40 per cent in the past 40 years, but instead of being dispersed across countryside these food units are increasingly concentrated into compact industrial blocks. The number of pigs has trebled to two billion. There are now two chickens for every human.

Industrialised food production has changed the world's diet, providing a cheap and plentiful form of protein. Yet it comes not only at a moral and environmental cost but also in terms of world health: the silent germs mutating and evolving amid the filth.

Factory farming is necessary to feed a hungry world. But doing so without also unleashing new diseases requires far more global co-operation on biosecurity, much tighter international regulation of the meat trade and, above all, a change in the way we produce animals for food. Mass-produced meat can kill you, even if you never eat it.

In 1953 British textbooks insisted that the war against germs had been won by antibiotics, declaring "the virtual elimination of infectious disease as a significant factor in social life". Accepting that premise, Michael Crichton's *The Andromeda Strain* imagined the world under assault from a microbe from outer space.

Today the world is once again under attack from infectious diseases. The latest plague does not come from God, or from other planets. It does not simply come from infectious animals and rogue microbes. It also comes from Man.

Factory Farming Contributes to Pfiesteria Outbreaks

Sierra Club

The Sierra Club, the oldest and largest environmental organization in the United States, works to protect communities, wild places, and the planet itself.

Pfiesteria piscicida is a microbe, a one-celled organism. Pfiesteria was first identified in 1991 by researchers at North Carolina State University.

Pfiesteria normally exists in a harmless state, but it can change into a form that may give off toxins that can kill fish and other aquatic life. Scientists have not yet determined what causes Pfiesteria to turn toxic.

Pfiesteria causes lesions in fish and has caused massive fish kills in rivers, including the Neuse River, where a 1995 outbreak killed 14 million fish and closed 364,000 acres of shellfish beds.

In Maryland, scientists have found fish with lesions similar to those caused by Pfiesteria in four rivers: the Pocomoke River, the Chicamacomico River and a branch of the Manokin River. Fish in Virginia's Rappahannock River have also been found with lesions. In Maryland, stretches of the three affected rivers have been closed. In the case of the Pocomoke river, the closure was ordered due to public health, not environmental concerns.

Fish affected have been both menhaden (not human food, used for oils, etc.) and sport fish species like striped bass. So far, there are no indications of harm to birds and other species, but concerns about human health for those exposed to water bodies remain.

Preliminary work done by physicians from Johns Hopkins University indicates ill effects in people who have had contact with water colonized by Pfiesteria. In North Carolina, physicians have reported skin ailments, memory loss and asthma-like symptoms, among other complaints, in more than 100 patients. It is not yet clear whether the harmful agent is only water-borne or may be transmitted by inhalation.

Why Are Pfiesteria Outbreaks Happening?

Nobody is sure—at least not yet. Pfiesteria seems to favor waters high in "nutrients" (nitrogen, phosphorus), but outbreaks aren't necessarily imminent in water-bodies with high nutrient levels. In addition, although the microbe usually grows in warmer waters, outbreaks have occurred in October and November, in cooler weather. "Activation" of the microbe often takes place in shallow water with poor circulation and with high concentrations of fish. However, "activation" has occurred in other water environments, too.

In the tidewater areas of Maryland, Delaware and Virginia ... farmers raise 600 million chickens, with about 24 pounds of waste per bird.

Though the causes of Pfiesteria outbreaks are not fully understood, in several cases scientists have linked the problem to polluted run-off as one factor. Polluted run-off—a scourge that affects many of our nation's waterways—comes from many sources. Programs to protect our water from run-off aren't always strong enough or adequately enforced.

In some states, run-off can be traced in part to high-density livestock raising operations. For example, in the tidewater areas of Maryland, Delaware and Virginia (known as the Del-Mar-Va peninsula), farmers raise 600 million chickens, with about 24 pounds of waste per bird. Although many operators are diligent about waste control, too much nitrogen leaves the land and ends up in the water, creating an environment where Pfiesteria can thrive. In North Carolina, industrial-sized hog farms may pose the same problem. North Carolina's hog population is approaching 10 million. And in 1995, 25 million gallons of pig manure—more than twice the volume of the Exxon Valdez spill—burst from a ruptured manure-storage facility into the New River.

Agriculture does contribute, but there are a myriad of other sources of "nutrients" or polluted run-off into the waterways. For example, fertilizers applied on home gardens and golf courses, auto emissions of nitrogen, and industries that refine oil or burn coal can also contribute.

Pfiesteria is front-page news in areas along the Atlantic Coast, but waterways choked by polluted run-off are problems that are national in scope. For example, along the Gulf Coast, citizens are growing more and more alarmed at the so-called Dead Zone, an area roughly the size of the state of Massachusetts, where low-oxygen waters make fish-kills commonplace, thereby devastating the commercial fishing and shrimping industries.

What Can We Do to Stop the Outbreaks?

The recent outbreaks of Pfiesteria only heighten Americans' concern about clean water, a concern that hasn't diminished in the 25 years since the Clean Water Act was signed. Although we've made strides in cutting pollution from industries, more needs to be done to keep waterways safe from polluted run-off.

Livestock farmers need to handle wastes in ways that protect our water, but it's everybody's responsibility to reduce pollution. Pollution prevention is the key. There are many sources of pollution burdening our rivers and coastal waters—from failing septic systems, to inadequate wastewater treatment plants, to boating and navigation, as well as agriculture and airborne pollution. Restoring overall health to our rivers, estuaries and bays will require concerted efforts to address those sources combined with protecting and restoring the wetlands and forested buffers that play such critical roles in filtering out pollutants, preventing them from flowing into our waterways. That's how we can help stop Pfiesteria in its tracks.

If we protect wetlands and forests near our waterways—instead of paving and developing open spaces—we'll help keep our waters safe.

Health Effects of Pfiesteria

The recent outbreaks of the Pfiesteria microbe have prompted great concern among citizens, particularly with regard to the health effects. Although scientists have not yet conclusively determined what causes outbreaks of the deadly form, the health impacts on wildlife have been quite clear. The toxic forms of Pfiesteria often attack fish, such as menhaden, causing the formation of skin lesions and ultimately death. Scientists believe that, in addition to severely impacting wildlife, the outbreaks may pose a threat to public health. Preliminary research investigating the human health effects reveals that the toxic form may lead to skin ailments, short-term memory loss, and asthma-like symptoms. Congress approved legislation on November 13th which allocates $5 million per year to universities researching Pfiesteria, and $13 million for research efforts at the Environmental Protection Agency, the Centers for Disease Control, and the National Oceanic and Atmospheric Administration. The agencies will study the human health effects more closely. Likewise, scientists at North Carolina University will pursue research to determine what initiates the toxic Pfiesteria forms and to understand more clearly how the toxins interact with humans.

Human Health Impacts

Researchers at North Carolina State University have personally experienced the harmful human health effects related to the toxic Pfeisteria....

Researchers studying the microbe are not the only ones who have suffered serious health effects from exposure to the toxins of Pfiesteria. The Maryland Department of Health and Mental Hygiene revealed on November 14th that 37 cases were reported in the Chesapeake Bay area of people suffering the symptoms of memory loss, skin rashes and lesions, and bouts of vomiting. Some of the affected persons were state officials taking water samples, boatsmen, fishermen, and a jet skier who came in contact with the water during a Pfiesteria outbreak.

Wildlife Health Impacts

A great deal of attention has been devoted to the wildlife health effects, particularly the fish illnesses and lesions. Some fish have experienced relatively mild lesions to the Pfiesteria attacks, while other fish populations have suffered more severe lesions. These links to the University System of Maryland Pfiesteria pages provide photographs and descriptions of the range of impacts on fish populations.

Technologies Soon Will Be Developed to Produce Meat Without Harm to the Environment

Kevin Slaten

Kevin Slaten is a junior fellow at the Carnegie Endowment for International Peace, a private, nonprofit organization dedicated to advancing cooperation among nations and promoting active international engagement by the United States.

Jim Motavalli [an environmental writer] recently predicted that the "vegetarian world" will be coming your way soon. Unhealthy, polluting, and simply impractical, meat won't be around much longer, he argues—at least not in a morally acceptable way.

The Benefits of Fish and Poultry

Let me be blunt: This is not our future. *Red* meat might well deserve probation, but fish and chicken are innocent of all charges. And even beef, lamb, and pork have their redeeming qualities—not least that technology might soon make them greenhouse gas free. So please, don't toss out your butcher's business card yet.

Motavalli offers two reasons why we ought to go veggie. First, he cites a study linking red meat consumption to cancer and heart disease. But alas, he seems to forget that there are tremendous differences between types of meat. Red meat is the only kind addressed in this study. And the Harvard School of Public Health claims that other meat sources (the ones that are low in saturated fat such as chicken or fish) *pose little risk to human health*. What's more, they might actually be good for you. Many fish are rich in the fatty acid docosahexaenoic acid, which *humans need* but bodies can't make themselves. Those omega-3s have become the latest "superfood," and—sorry, vegetarians—they cannot be found anywhere else in nature. A person who eats fish is *less* likely to have heart disease than someone who doesn't—say, a vegetarian.

The vegetarian revolution appears to be neither essential nor likely.

Next, Motavalli warns us that meat contributes more to greenhouse gases (GHG) than the entire transportation sector. But here again, he fails to differentiate between different types of livestock. True, the industry overall may emit 18 percent of all GHG, but the beef sector emits 13 times as much as the poultry sector, meaning that chicken production contributes no more than 1 percent to global GHG. Compare that with a vegetarian favorite—rice—which *emits 1.5 percent of climate-heating gases.*

No Vegetarian Revolution

Despite all of this variation, Motavalli declares, "The obvious solution to both health and environmental disasters is to stop eating meat altogether." Actually, that choice will be a moot point in just 15 years, he argues: "By 2025, we simply won't have the resources" to keep eating meat. With growing demand for resource-intensive animal products, vegetarianism seems inevitable.

Again, I beg to differ. This prediction rests on the bizarre assumption that technology will stagnate. The reality is quite the opposite. Scientists are refining methods for growing meat tissue in the lab without the costs of land, water, and feed, whose use inflicts so much environmental collateral damage. They call it *in vitro meat*, and even the veggie-lovers love it.

Last year, the animal rights group PETA [People for the Ethical Treatment of Animals] even *offered a $1 million prize* to the "first person to come up with a method to produce commercially viable quantities of in vitro meat at competitive prices by 2012."

So, upon closer inspection, the vegetarian revolution appears to be neither essential nor likely.

None of this means that we should ignore the pressing threat of climate change. But the plan of action need not be as bombastic as cutting out an entire section of the food pyramid. At the policy level, a carbon cap could tax the worst polluters in the livestock industry. Meanwhile, more money should be invested in technologies like in vitro meat and methane capture and storage. As consumers, we should think about diversifying our sources of dietary protein, eating less beef and pork and more dairy, poultry, fish, and soy.

Climate control and public health are critical for our collective future, but both are damaged by inaccuracies and half-truths. Vegetarianism is not the impending reality. Technology and good old common sense will allow us to have our meat . . . and eat it too.

In Vitro Meat Production Could Provide a Sustainable Way to Produce Meat

Stig Omholt

Stig Omholt is a professor at the Centre for Integrative Genetics, Norwegian University of Life Sciences.

According to the Food and Agricultural Organization of the United Nations' recent report "Livestock's long shadow—environmental issues and options", global production of meat is projected to more than double from 229×10^9 kg/year in 1999/2000 to 465×10^9 kg/year in 2050. The bulk of growth will occur in developing countries through intensive production systems where economies of scale will cause a steady increase of the size of operations. It is expected that the future growth of livestock output will be based on similar growth rates for feed concentrate use.

The Problems with Meat Production

The total area occupied by livestock grazing is around 34×10^6 km², which is equivalent to 26% of the land surface area of the planet. The total area used for feedcrop production is about 4.7x106 km², equivalent to 33% of all cropland. Most of this cropland is located in OECD [Organization for Economic Cooperation and Development] countries, but some developing countries are rapidly expanding their feedcrop production, notably maize and soybean in South America, in particular Brazil. The total remaining area suitable for grain-fed production is estimated to be about 28×10^6 km², of which 45% is forest area. Livestock contribute about 9% of total carbon dioxide emissions, 37% of methane and 65% of nitrous oxide.

In terms of CO_2 [carbon dioxide] equivalents the gaseous emissions from livestock production amount to about 18% of the global warming effects. This is more than the contribution from the total transportation sector. Concerning polluting gaseous emissions not linked to climate change, livestock waste contributes 68% of total emissions of ammonia ($30x10^9$ kg/ year). About $0.13x10^6$ km^2 of forest is lost per year and the majority is converted to agricultural land.

Besides the environmental impact of meat production, large scale farming and worldwide transport of livestock and animal products have contributed to a surge of infectious diseases that not only affect animals but also pose a threat to humans all over the world. Moreover, in Western societies there is an increasing concern about the animal welfare issues attached to industrialized production where normal economic principles force the development of production routines where living animals are treated as inanimate capitalistic commodities.

[In vitro meat] . . . may allow development of a down-sized animal production industry . . . that . . . is ecologically sound and meets basic animal welfare requirements.

In a business as usual perspective: (i) the spatial and commercial concentration of livestock production will continue to grow, (ii) the pressure on crop agriculture to expand will remain high, and the associated environmental impacts, in terms of deforestation, water depletion, climate change and biodiversity loss, will grow, (iii) livestock contribution to anthropogenic greenhouse gas emissions will increase, and (iv) livestock-induced degradation of the world's arid and semi-arid lands will continue, in particular in Africa and South and Central Asia.

In Vitro Meat Production Possibilities

It is a tremendous political and economic challenge to change this grim scenario into a more sustainable one if we continue to base our meat consumption solely on production of animals. It will demand sacrifices that are probably well beyond what will be accepted by the majority of citizens in developed countries. One way to get out of this predicament is to exploit the potential of modern biotechnology and process technology to produce meat from normal muscle progenitor cells in bioreactors at an industrial scale. If this production strategy were to replace a substantial part of the current meat production regime, this may allow development of a downsized animal production industry which can acquire a competitive edge in the upper-level meat market by documenting that it is ecologically sound and meets basic animal welfare requirements.

An environmentally friendly cultured meat technology rests on four basic premises: (1) the culturing of stem cells from farm animals of choice that are able to proliferate at a high rate but that do not differentiate, (2) the efficient differentiation of these stem cells into muscle cells that contain all nutrients present in conventional meat, (3) the application of a growth medium that does not contain animal products, and (4) the organisation of the muscle cells into 3-dimensional muscle structures.

CHAPTER 4

What Is the Future of Factory Farming?

Chapter Preface

According to the Humane Society of the United States (HSUS), about ten billion animals are raised and slaughtered each year by the meat, egg, and dairy industries, the majority of which use factory farming methods. However, the main federal law affecting animal welfare—the Animal Welfare Act, which mandates minimal humane care, handling, treatment, and transportation of certain animals (including lab animals, animals raised by dog and cat breeders, and zoo and circus animals)—does not apply to farm animals. The only federal law that does apply to farm animals is the Humane Methods of Slaughter Act, but this law excludes poultry, which makes up a large part of the farm animal population. Also, although every state has an animal cruelty law, most states exempt common factory farming practices. Yet despite this history of non-protection, the past five years have seen many successful efforts at the state level to pass legislation or initiatives designed to provide better legal safeguards for farm animals. The past two years were the most prolific, according to the HSUS, with eighty-six new animal protection laws enacted in 2007 and ninety-three in 2008.

Many of these new laws targeted specific practices that have been standard in factory farms for decades. In 2002, for example, Florida voters approved a ballot initiative that banned hog gestation crates—a factory farming practice of keeping pregnant hogs in small metal pens that prevent sows from turning around or comfortably lying down. In 2006, Arizona voters approved a similar initiative to ban pig gestation crates as well as veal crates—similar, small crates that prevent young calves from turning around, stretching their limbs, or lying down in a comfortable position. Oregon's legislature followed the example set by Florida and Arizona voters and banned pig gestation crates in 2007. In May 2008, Colorado joined the trend by enacting legislation to permanently phase out both gestation crates and veal crates, followed by Maine, which enacted similar legislation in 2009.

Probably the most ambitious effort to help farm animals, however, was Proposition 2, the Prevention of Farm Animal Cruelty Act, in California—a 2008 ballot measure adopted by a wide margin of more than 63 percent of the state's voters. The measure, promoted by HSUS, prohibits the confinement of a farm animal for a majority of the day in a way that prevents it from lying down, standing up, fully extending its limbs, or turning around freely. Proposition 2 prevents the crating of veal calves and breeding pigs, as other states have done, but because California has relatively few beef and hog producers, it mainly affects the caging of egg-laying hens. Egg producers and other opponents fought the measure, claiming it would cause egg prices to rise precipitously and that cage-free hens would be more susceptible to bird flu. Voters rejected these arguments, sending a clear message of concern about the plight of farm animals. As a result, the new law is expected to change the face of the California egg industry. Reportedly, more than 90 percent of the state's 20 million egg-laying hens are kept in battery cages, stacked one upon the other. Although it is not yet clear how Proposition 2 will be interpreted, the measure will require egg producers to raise and manage birds without putting them in tiny cages whose surface area is about the size of a standard sheet of paper— currently the industry norm. The new requirements, however, do not take effect until 2015.

The California initiative and voters' strong show of support for alleviating the suffering of food-producing animals has inspired state legislators to consider a number of other animal welfare measures. In 2009, California legislators introduced bills that would ban docking the tails of milk cows (amputation of up to two-thirds of the tail, typically performed without anesthetic, to improve cleanliness), stop the import of out-of-state eggs from hens kept in cages, and ban the practice of feeding antibiotics to farm animals, along with various other animal welfare measures that affect other animals, such as pets and wildlife. Legislators have noted that about eight million Californians voted for Proposition 2, the most votes won for any citizen initiative in the state's history. Many policymakers believe that it marks an important change in attitude about the treatment of farm animals among the voting public.

Animal welfare advocates are now hoping to fund initiatives similar to California's Proposition 2 in other states. Two states under consideration are Ohio and Michigan, both of which are home to large meat and dairy companies. Legislators in these two states, however, are opposing animal welfare proposals and instead introducing legislation that would establish third-party boards that would be given authority for regulating livestock and poultry care and welfare. Meanwhile, a bill titled the Prevention of Farm Animal Cruelty Act has already been introduced in Rhode Island's legislature with the same language and title of the California initiative.

At the federal level, the most significant proposal is a bill called the Preservation of Antibiotics for Medical Treatment Act of 2009 (PAMTA), which has been introduced in both the House and the Senate. If passed, the law would ban the use of antibiotics important to human health on factory farms unless animals are sick.

If these new laws and proposals signify a trend toward improving conditions for farm animals, factory farming may be forced to change significantly in future years and decades. The authors of the viewpoints in this chapter set forth various visions of the future for factory agriculture and animal production, many of them concerned with another important issue, environmental sustainability.

Commercial Agriculture Will Continue to Play a Role in Future Agriculture Policy

George McGovern and Marshall Matz

George McGovern is a former U.S. representative and senator from South Dakota and the unsuccessful Democratic presidential nominee in 1972. As senator, McGovern was chairman of the Senate Select Committee on Nutrition and Human Needs and an important legislator in areas of U.S. farming and agriculture. Marshall Matz was the general counsel for the Senate Select Committee on Nutrition and Human Needs while McGovern served as its chairman. They both are on the board of directors of the World Food Program, the food aid branch of the United Nations.

President-elect Barack Obama has chosen Iowa's former Gov. Tom Vilsack to be his secretary of agriculture. Vilsack was an excellent choice, but some have criticized the appointment because he supports agricultural biotechnology and commercial agriculture. The critics assume that anyone who holds these views is an enemy of organic farming and sustainable agriculture. We disagree.

Feeding the World

Norman Borlaug, a Nobel laureate and father of the Green Revolution, has concluded that the world will have to produce more food in the next 50 years than it has in the last 10,000. That is an extraordinary challenge. How does the world do it?

First, we must recognize that organic, sustainable and commercial agriculture play a part in feeding the world. There is an important role for organic agriculture and, indeed, some

George McGovern and Marshall Matz, "Agriculture's Next Big Challenge," *Chicago Tribune*, January 4, 2009. Reproduced by permission of the authors.

consumers are willing to pay a premium for foods that are certified as organic. Sustainable agriculture, defined generally as farming that adheres to practices more sensitive to the environment, is also of great importance. Commercial agriculture is still the backbone of the economy in most rural counties across the nation. And commercial agriculture is a big factor in offsetting our unfavorable balance of international trade.

We do not yet see the yields with organic agriculture that would feed a hungry planet of almost 7 billion people. During the recent presidential campaign, Obama, to his credit, often talked of supporting American agriculture, from the small sustainable farms that market to the community to the large commercial farms that feed the world. He was exactly correct. The Department of Agriculture should be supporting research into organic and sustainable agriculture. Clearly, we must be more sensitive to the relationship between agriculture and the environment. But to criticize someone for supporting all sectors of agriculture seems shortsighted.

The Future of Agriculture

When we look to the future of agriculture we see these challenges:

- The primary goal of agriculture is to feed ourselves and those around the globe who lack America's productive resources.

- We must not forget those who receive assistance through school breakfast and lunch programs, food stamps and nutritional supplements for low-income pregnant and nursing mothers and their young children. In poor, developing countries, more food assistance is needed to support the fight against AIDS.

- Agriculture is key in our becoming less dependent on foreign oil by converting crops into biofuels and renewal energy.

- We must accomplish the first three goals without plowing up environmentally fragile land.

America's farmers have become so efficient that 1 percent of the population can feed the entire country and much of the world. One of the downsides of this efficiency is that consumers have forgotten where our food comes from and what it takes to get our bounty into supermarkets.

We all want a safe, ubiquitous and inexpensive food supply. Even with the recent food price inflation, Americans still spend only 10 percent of their disposable income on food, the lowest in the world. A case can be made that our entire consumer economy is fueled by cheap food. There would not be as many cell phones and other conveniences if Americans had to spend 20 percent or more of their disposable income on food.

We need to get beyond ideology and depend more on science. We need to develop a new understanding of agriculture based on our larger goals if we are to craft a long-term food and farm policy that works. Agriculture has a responsibility to adjust and contribute to improving the environment. But let's stick to science and avoid an ideological debate about agricultural practices.

Industrial Agriculture Must Be Carefully Regulated in the Future

Will Allen

Will Allen is a leading organic farmer in the United States and a member of the Policy Advisory Board of the Organic Consumers Association.

Taxpayers are demanding that government enforce existing regulations and create more stringent rules to limit the excess and greed in banking, insurance, housing, and on Wall Street. But, in the rush to regulate, we can't forget to oversee industrial agriculture. It is one of our most polluting and dangerous industries. Like the financial sectors, its practices have not been well regulated for the last thirty years. Let me run down a few of the major problems that have developed because of our poorly regulated U.S. agriculture.

Carbon Foot Print

The U.S. EPA [Environmental Protection Agency] estimated in 2007 that agriculture in the U.S. was responsible for about 18% of our carbon footprint, which is huge because the U.S. is the largest polluter in the world. This should include (but doesn't) the manufacture and use of pesticides and fertilizers, fuel and oil for tractors, equipment, trucking and shipping, electricity for lighting, cooling, and heating, and emissions of carbon dioxide, methane, nitrous oxide and other green house gases. Unfortunately, the EPA estimate of 18% still doesn't include a large portion of the fuel, the synthetic nitrogen fertilizer, some of the nitrous oxide, all of the CFCs [chlorofluorocarbons] and bromines, and most of the transport emissions. When they are counted, agriculture's share of the U.S. carbon footprint will be at least 25 to 30%.

Factory farming is polluting the ground, river, and ocean water with high amounts of nitrogen, phosphorous, and other fertilizers.

Oftentimes we see all greenhouse gasses as being equivalent to carbon dioxide (CO_2). But, methane emissions are 21 times and nitrous oxides 310 times more damaging as greenhouse gasses than CO_2. Since agriculture is one of the largest producers of methane and nitrous oxide, the extent of the agricultural impact is staggering. Unless we change our bad habits of food production and long distance delivery, we will not be able to deal with climate change.

Fertilizer Pollution/Dead Zones

Factory farming is polluting the ground, river, and ocean water with high amounts of nitrogen, phosphorous, and other fertilizers. High levels of nitrates and nitrites were found in twenty-five thousand community wells that provided drinking water to two thirds of the nation's population. More than fifteen million people in two hundred eighty communities are drinking water with phosphorous or phosphates which mostly come from industrial farming operations.

Nitrate and phosphorous fertilizer runoff flow into the rivers and ultimately end up in the ocean. The river water rides up over the heavier salt water when it reaches the ocean and algae blooms develop on the fertilizer rich water. When the algae die, the bacteria use up all of the oxygen in decomposing them. This creates an oxygen dead (or hypoxic) zone. In 1995, scientists identified 60 dead zones around the world.

Recent results published in 2008 identified 405 oceanic dead zones. The prime cause for dead zones is the use of highly soluble synthetic fertilizers, which are overused to obtain maximum yields. The government regulations on the total maximum daily load (tmdl) of synthetic nitrogen, or phosphorous fertilizer coming off of farms were established under the Clean Water Act. But those statutes are routinely not enforced. There are exceptions, but in general the regulators have been in a thirty-year coma. . . .

Factory farmers continue to use enormous quantities of the most toxic poisons. In 2006, four of the six most used farm pesticides in California were among the most dangerous chemicals in the world. Farmers applied more than 35.7 million pounds of four pesticides: Metam sodium, Methyl bromide, Telone II, and Chloropicrin. . . .

In 2004, California Strawberry growers used 184 pesticides. They applied an average of more than 335 pounds of pesticides per acre. Metam sodium, methyl bromide, chloropicrin and Telone II accounted for 74% (or 248 pounds) of the pesticides used on each acre of strawberries. Four of the world's most toxic chemicals accounted for almost three-quarters of all pesticides used. Strawberry shortcake, anyone?

California is the only state that has collected pesticide use data in the U.S. (New York recently passed the same law). Unfortunately, for all the other states, we do not have good data. California began collecting use data from farmers and applicators in 1970. The USDA [U.S. Department of Agriculture] and most states only collect survey data, not actual usage amounts. Because California has real data, and because California provides half of the fresh produce in the country, their information is an invaluable guide to the level of poisonous exposure that U.S. farmers, farmworkers, food handlers, and customers have endured on farm products for almost forty years. . . .

Confinement Animals/Excess Antibiotics and Hormones

I have pointed out in *The War on Bugs* and in other articles that our confinement animal operations (where most of our meat comes from) are a serious health and safety threat. And, as we have all come to realize, they are very poorly regulated. Overuse of hormones and antibiotics has left us with antibiotic resistant meat, large quantities of antibiotics in rivers and drinking water, and even antibiotic resistant pork farmers and consumers. Beef cows are often injected with hormones, milk cows with genetically modified growth hormones. The U.S. meat supply is so dangerously unhealthy that large amounts of it are regularly recalled (about 200,000,000 pounds of beef in 2008) and some of the more suspicious or contaminated meat has been allowed by the FDA [Food and Drug Administration] to be irradiated since the 1990s. Naked meat?

We raised 11 billion meat, milk, and egg-laying animals in the U.S. in 2008. By 2008, we produced nearly 69 million pigs, 95% in confinement. We raised 300 million commercial laying hens in battery cages, Ten billion meat chickens, and half a billion turkeys were confined in abusive close quarter conditions. About 33 million beef cows and 9.7 million dairy cows spent their dreary days in disgusting feedlots and dairy barns. These facilities and their meat products are rife with disease that the public is advised to combat by thorough cooking. In December, 2008 *Consumer Reports* found that 83% of the 525 meat chickens they studied had salmonella or campylobacter. With deadly diseases on all but 17 chickens out of 100, customers are asking: What about the salmonella on my drain board or my hands? No wonder there is so much food borne illness!

These enormous populations of animals also produce a lot of manure, and massive amounts of methane and nitrous oxide. The largest amount of nitrous oxide comes from fertilizer used on farmland that produces feed for confined animals. High methane emissions come from mountains of animal manure and digestive gasses, and a lesser though significant amount, from unsustainable grazing. Seventy to eighty percent of our farm production and acreage is used to produce the aforementioned 11 billion beef cows, pigs, poultry, milk cows, sheep, and goats. Fertilizer use in the U.S. is variable depending on the needs of the crop and the natural fertility of the land. Corn and cotton farmers, who grow the corn and cottonseed to feed these confined animals, use 200 to 300 pounds of nitrogen per acre and about 100 pounds of phosphorous. This is much more nitrogen and phosphorous than the crops can use in a single season, but the farmers are advised to use "enough" to get the highest possible yields. So, most of the nitrogen and phosphorous fertilizer that the plants don't need and can't use are flushed into rivers, lakes and the ocean.

U.S. factory farming can't be fixed.

I could continue further with this litany of unregulated farm problems, but these are the major issues. We are living in a very polluted and dangerous food world, partly because of the unregulated excesses of U.S. industrial farming. If we are going to bring down our high rates of obesity, diabetes, heart disease, cancer, and birth defects we have to change our food choices and how that food is raised. Besides creating profound health and safety problems, industrial farming is a huge unregulated contributor to global warming and an enormous user of energy. We must regulate and significantly reduce the U.S. farm use of fuels, pesticides, and fertilizer. These are not choices! These are necessities! If we are going to seriously tackle climate change and fix our health system, we have to change our form of agriculture.

We Can't Fix Factory Farming!

The Pew Charitable Trusts and the Johns-Hopkins Bloomberg School of Public Health conducted a study in 2008 and determined that the U.S. factory farming system is dangerously out of control and that many practices, including animal confinement, and the prophylactic [preventive]-use of antibiotics and hormones must be phased out. A second study, also in April of 2008, by the Union of Concerned Scientists concluded much the same. Both studies found that the current factory farming paradigms are simply not sustainable for the land, the drinking water, the confined animals, the rivers, and the oceans, and they are seriously damaging our public health. The Union of Concerned Scientists reminded us that we will be subsidizing these bad farming practices once again on April 15th when we pay our taxes. That is the second payment for "cheap food".

For more than one hundred years U.S. and European safe food activists demanded real regulation of farm chemicals. But, it was always a pipe dream, since chemical firms, the universities and the government all alleged that the pesticides were safe and that farmers couldn't get good yields without chemicals. So, the regulators looked the other way. However, farmers around the world have demonstrated that they can produce as good or better yields of quality food and fiber without dangerous and damaging chemicals. Still, the regulators continue to look the other way and still refuse to stop the poisoning.

Salmonella contaminated pistachios, peanuts, tomatoes, melons, and jalapenos and the slaughtering of downer beef are glaring examples of sloppy farming and processing combined with regulatory failure. All of these regulatory failures and bad farming practices didn't just cause bankruptcy or a huge cut in 401-Ks, they sickened hundreds of millions and killed hundreds of thousands of people over the last thirty years!

Each day seems to bring more pesticide spills and injuries, more poisoned food, more contaminated drinking water, more dead zones and more residues on our food. Consequently, immediate regulation of and a rapid phase-out of the most toxic farm chemicals now seem like urgencies, instead of pipe dreams.

If We Can't Fix It, Let's Change It!

While U.S. factory farming can't be fixed, the good news is that changing U.S. agriculture is not an unattainably complex goal. However, it does call for a paradigm shift. We must stop pretending that fossil based fertilizer and fuel is endless, sustainable, or environmentally justifiable. The Green Revolution is over! After one hundred years of use the jury is in. What looked in 1909 like a cheap and efficient fertilizer has polluted our drinking water, turned deadly to the oceans, is increasingly more expensive, and today is doing more harm than good. We must dramatically reduce the use of synthetic nitrogen fertilizer and begin an immediate phase out.

In 1945, only five percent of the nitrogen used on U.S. farms was synthetic. Now, more than ninety-five percent is. Before the synthetic takeover, farmers grew fertilizer crops and applied small amounts of composted manure for fertility and tilth [cultivation], to increase organic matter, and to feed the microorganisms. These techniques and more modern ones are used by both organic and non-organic farmers today and enable them to produce high yields of quality produce, meat, fiber, oilseeds, and grains. Farmers all over the world are getting higher yields of calories per acre on diversified organic farms than on monocultural chemical or GMO [genetically modified organism] farms.

We can solve the dead zone problem by switching back from synthetic nitrogen and soluble phosphorous fertilizers to organic plant-based fertility. This is not rocket science and it is not a long shot with outmoded technology. It is, in fact, achievable within a few years. As a plus, fertilizer crops sequester carbon, which our currently barren soils in the fall and winter don't.

We can eliminate the cancer and birth defect clusters and high pesticide residues on our favorite foods by using . . . strategies to control pests and diseases. Releasing beneficial insects, altering our growing practices, rotation of crops, soil balancing, and careful monitoring of pest damage are a few of the successful techniques that thousands of farmers are using to control pests and eliminate poisonous pesticides on their farms.

This is a challenging time for farmers, with many sorting out how can they produce their own energy on the farm as well as auditing and reducing their use. Most of us know that the cheap era of fossil fuel is over. With agriculture being responsible for such a large percentage of fossil fuel consumption, it is essential that resources be invested in alternative energy strategies by farmers, entrepreneurs, and by state and federal government agencies.

At this critical juncture, we should see these factory farm problems and their solutions as an opportunity. This is an opportunity for us to demand that Washington regulate our food supply. It is a chance to make real changes in our own diets by eating safe foods, supporting local organic farms, and frequenting farmers markets. Additionally, each of us can grow chemically free vegetables and fruits in our own yards, like the Obamas are doing at the White House.

It is also a time of opportunity to assist farmers and merchants in converting U.S. farming and the food system. To do this, we need much more government investment in the reinvigoration of our agricultural extension service. These new or retrained extension agents would help farmers make the transition to sustainable and organic agriculture (as some currently are). We also need access for young and not so young farmers to financial aid and government held farmland. Clearly, we also need lots more regulators. Only the government can address these issues. But, we must pressure the [President Barack] Obama run EPA, USDA, and FDA to address them as if they were urgent.

U.S. organic farmers developed a set of standards in the 1970s and 1980s to regulate farms and farmers with third party inspections. They did this to assure a suspicious public that the food they produced was really organic. The standards they enforce require crop rotation, an organic fertility and pest control program and prohibit the use of toxic fertilizers, chemical pesticides, hormones, antibiotics, genetic modification, sewage sludge, irradiation, and the feeding of animal protein to animals.

"Conventional" food in the U.S can be grown with all the farming practices outlawed in organic. Conventional is a semantic ploy to avoid calling the food "chemical", or "poisonous". Whatever you call it, it should be regulated and the most damaging practices should be made illegal.

Finally, we need to internationally harmonize our regulations, so that there is as much unanimity to the rules as possible and the enforcement is transparent. This is just as important in food as it is in finance. We are all too connected globally to pretend that we should not worry about another culture's food regulations or health concerns. Ideally, we should all embrace a more rigorous international REACH-like program that would protect farmers, farmworkers, processors and consumers. Hopefully, the Obama administration attitude toward regulation will extend to U.S. agriculture. If it doesn't, we are in deep shit! And, I'm not talking manure.

Industrial Animal Agriculture Must Transition to a More Sustainable System

Pew Commission on Industrial Farm Animal Production

The Pew Commission on Industrial Farm Animal Production is a group of experts from various fields formed to conduct a comprehensive, fact-based, and balanced examination of key aspects of the U.S. farm animal industry.

Sustainability is a futuristic concept. *Webster's* dictionary defines the verb "sustain" as "to maintain," "to keep in existence," "to keep going." By definition, then, sustainability is a journey, an ongoing process, not a prescription or a set of instructions. So when we ask, "How do we sustain animal agriculture?" we are asking how to manage animal agriculture so that it can be maintained indefinitely and what changes are necessary to accomplish that goal.

Sustainable animal agriculture requires that we envision the challenges and changes the future will bring. In his extensive studies of past civilizations, [author] Jared Diamond has observed that civilizations that correctly assessed their current situations, anticipated changes, and started preparing for those changes were the ones that thrived—they were sustainable. Civilizations that failed in these efforts were the ones that collapsed—they were not sustainable.

What is true for civilizations is likely also true for business enterprises. So this report would not be complete without an assessment of some of the changes likely to emerge in the decades ahead and recommendations to address those changes.

Putting Meat on the Table: Industrial Farm Animal Production in America. Washington, DC: Pew Commission on Industrial Farm Animal Production, 2008. Copyright © 2006 The Pew Commission on Industrial Farm Animal Production. All rights reserved. Reproduced by permission.

Changes Ahead

To begin, it is important to recognize that our food production system today operates in the general framework of the industrial economy, which begins from the assumptions that natural resources and other inputs to fuel economic activities are unlimited and that nature provides unlimited sinks to absorb the wastes thrown off by that economic activity. Our modern food system, including industrial animal agriculture, is part of that economy.

[Economist] Herman E. Daly has warned for some time that this economy is not sustainable, that we must recognize that human economies are *subsystems* of larger ecosystems and must adapt to function within ecosystem constraints. Because the natural resources that have fueled our food and agriculture systems are now in a state of depletion and nature's sinks are saturated, Daly's prediction may soon be realized. . . .

Most climatologists . . . agree that greater climate fluctuations—"extremes of precipitation, both droughts and floods"—are likely.

Among the many changes likely in the next 50 years, we believe the following three will be especially challenging to the US industrial food and agriculture system: the depletion of stored *energy* and *water* resources, and changing *climate*. These changes will be especially challenging because America's successful industrial economy of the past century was based on the availability of *cheap* energy, a relatively *stable* climate, and *abundant* fresh water, and current methods have assumed the continued availability of these resources.

The End of Cheap Energy

The end of cheap energy may well be the first limited resource to force change in industrial food animal production as IFAP [industrial farm animal production] systems are almost entirely dependent on fossil fuels. The nitrogen used for fertilizer to produce animal feed is derived from natural gas. Phosphorus and potash are mined, processed, and transported to farms with petroleum energy. Pesticides are manufactured from petroleum resources. Farm equipment is manufactured and operated with petroleum energy. Feed is produced and trucked to concentrated animal operations with fossil fuels. Manure is collected and hauled to distant locations with fossil fuels.

When fossil fuels were cheap, these inputs to the process of agricultural production were available at very low cost. But independent scholars agree that oil production either already has peaked or will shortly do so. . . .

The depletion of fossil fuel resources will require that America transition not only to *alternative* fuels to produce food but to a new energy *system*.

Over 70% of global fresh water resources is used for [crop] irrigation.

The real energy transition will have to be from an energy *input* system to an energy *exchange* system, and this transition is likely to entail significant system changes in the US production of crops and livestock. For example, future agricultural production systems are less likely to be specialized monocultures and more likely to be based on biological diversity, organized so that each organism exchanges energy with other organisms, forming a web of synchronous relationships, instead of relying on energy-intensive inputs.

The End of Stable Climate

A second natural resource that has been essential to industrial agriculture is a relatively *stable climate*. We often mistakenly attribute the yield-producing success of the past century entirely to the development of new production technologies. But those robust yields were due at least as much to unusually favorable climate conditions as they were to technology.

A National Academy of Sciences (NAS) Panel on Climatic Variation reported in 1975 that "our present [stable] climate is in fact highly *abnormal*" and that "the earth's climate has always been changing, and the magnitude of . . . the changes can be catastrophic" (emphasis added). The report went on to suggest that climate change might be exacerbated by "our own activities" and concluded that "the global patterns of food production and population that have evolved are *implicitly dependent* on the climate of the present century". In other words, according to the NAS, it is this *combination* of "normal" climate variation *plus* the changes caused by industrial economies (greenhouse gas emissions) that could have a significant impact on future agricultural productivity.

While most climatologists acknowledge that it is impossible to predict exactly how climate change will affect agricultural production in the near term, they agree that greater climate fluctuations—"extremes of precipitation, both droughts and floods"—are likely. Such instability can be especially devastating for the highly specialized, genetically uniform, monoculture systems characteristic of current industrial crop and livestock production.

The End of Abundant Water

A third natural resource that may challenge our current agricultural production system is *water*. [Environmentalist] Lester Brown points out that although each human needs only four liters of water a day, the US industrial agriculture system consumes 2,000 liters per day to meet US daily food requirements. A significant amount of that water is consumed by production agriculture: over 70% of global fresh water resources is used for irrigation.

The Ogallala Aquifer, which supplies water for one of every five irrigated acres in the United States, is now half depleted and is being overdrawn at the rate of 3.1 trillion gallons per year, according to some reports. Furthermore, a recent *Des Moines Register* article reported that the production of biofuels is putting significant additional pressure on US water resources, and that climate change is likely to further stress these resources. . . .

Keys to Sustainability

These early indications of stress indicate that energy, water, and climate changes will intersect and affect each other in many ways and will make industrial production systems increasingly vulnerable.

Current intensive confined animal feeding operations can take steps to begin transitioning to a more sustainable future.

But new soil management methods can make major contributions to the sustainability of future US farming systems. Research and on-farm experience have shown that the management of soils in accordance with closed recycling systems that build soil organic matter significantly enhances the soil's capacity to absorb and retain moisture, reducing the need for irrigation. On-farm experience (as well as nature's own elasticity) also indicates that: (1) diverse systems are more resilient than monocultures in the face of adverse climate conditions; (2) energy inputs can be dramatically reduced when recycling systems replace input/output systems; and (3) management of soil health based on recycling systems requires more mixed crop/livestock systems. Furthermore, new insights from studies in modern ecology and evolutionary biology applied to nutrient recycling and humus-based soil management could provide additional information that can help in the design of postindustrial farming systems. . . .

The management of pests, weeds, or animal diseases from such an ecological perspective involves a web of relationships that require more biologically diverse systems. . . . In short, natural system management can revitalize soil health, reduce weed and other pest pressures, eliminate the need for pesticides, and support the transition from an energy-intensive industrial farming operation to a self-regulating, self-renewing one. A diversified crop/animal system enhances the possibilities for establishing a self-regulating system.

Other benefits, such as greater water conservation, follow from the improved soil health that results from closed recycling systems. As research conducted by John Reganold and his colleagues has demonstrated, soil managed by such recycling methods develops richer top soil, more than twice the organic matter, more biological activity, and far greater moisture absorption and holding capacity.

Such soil management methods illustrate the path to an energy system that operates on the basis of energy *exchange* instead of energy *input*. But more innovation is needed. Nature, for example, is a very efficient energy manager; all of its energy comes from sunlight, which is processed into carbon through photosynthesis and becomes available to various organisms that exchange energy through a web of relationships. Bison on the prairie obtain their energy from the grass, which gets its energy from the soil. Bison deposit their excrement on the grass and thus provide energy for insects and other organisms, which, in turn, convert it to energy that enriches the soil to produce more grass. These are the energy exchange systems that must be explored and adapted for use in postindustrial farming systems. But very little research is currently devoted to exploring such energy exchanges for farms.

Fortunately, a few farmers have already developed energy exchange systems and appear to be quite successful in managing their operations with very little fossil fuel input. But converting farms to this new energy model on a national scale will require a major transformation. The highly specialized, energy-intensive monocultures will need to convert to complex, highly diversified operations that function on energy exchange. Research has established the practicality and multiple benefits of such integrated crop-livestock operations, but further research is needed to explore how to adapt this new model of farming to various climates and ecosystems.

More Sustainable Animal Production

In the meantime, current intensive confined animal feeding operations can take steps to begin transitioning to a more sustainable future. In our visits to many such operations, we saw innovative adaptations of some of these principles. For example, a large feedlot we visited, which holds 90,000 head of cattle in confinement, composts all of its manure and sells it in a thriving compost market, thus improving its bottom line. As fertilizer costs go up due to increased energy costs, more farmers may turn to such sources of fertilizer to reduce their costs. The Commission visited an integrated producer of 90,000 dozen eggs a day, that composts its manure, mixing it with wood chips from ground-up wooden pallets, and sells the compost as garden and landscaping mulch, again generating additional income for the company. A 4,500-cow confinement dairy operation recycles its bedding sand and plastic baling wire. Both the dairy and the feedlot also cover their silage piles to reduce pollution.

Farmers in many parts of the world are adopting deep-bedded hoop barn technologies for raising their animals in confinement. Hoop barns are much less expensive to construct, have demonstrated production efficiencies comparable to those of nonbedded confinement systems, and are more welfare-friendly for animals. The deep-bedded systems allow animals to exercise more of their natural functions, absorb urine and manure for composting and building soil quality on nearby land, and provide warmth for the animals in cold weather. Such hoop structures are used in hog, beef, dairy, and some poultry operations and have demonstrated reduced environmental impact and risk.

Tweaking the current monoculture confinement operations with such methods will be very useful in the short term, but as energy, water, and climate resources undergo dramatic changes, it is the Commission's judgment that US agricultural production will need to transition to much more biologically diverse systems, organized into biological synergies that exchange energy, improve soil quality, and conserve water and other resources. As Herman Daly said, long-term sustainability will require a transformation from an industrial economy to an ecological economy.

The World Must Abandon the Commodity Approach to Food

Greg Bowman

Greg Bowman is the communications manager for the Rodale Institute, a nonprofit organization that promotes organic agriculture.

Agribusiness and grain-trade policy as usual is being challenged around the world in light of 2008's global food shortages and persistent hunger in many sectors. A new theme is that free-trade rules and international banking mandates to developing nations are failing, food-wise.

The Commodity Model's Failures

The commodity agriculture model has evolved to require staple grain crops to be grown as efficiently as possible in one place for export to the highest buyer outside the country. This approach has too often made farming into an industrial process while rendering the role of feeding the cultivated land's people into a virtual afterthought. Political leaders, researchers and grassroots agricultural organizations are increasingly in agreement that transition to more organic farming methods that target feeding their home areas first will build stronger, safer and ultimately more prosperous countries.

Six years ago, African leaders agreed to an initiative to focus agriculture-based development to end hunger, reduce poverty and food insecurity along with increasing opportunities for export. Results have been minimal and measures imprecise, but the goals are in place.

In contemporary research that factors in human health, ecological restoration, environmental responsibility and sustainability tied to current solar power, the current yield-focused conventional farming practices come up short. Dramatic price dips for crude oil notwithstanding, fossil fuels are no longer a sustainable foundation for food production.

Compared with biologically based systems of crop and livestock production, input-dependent systems that demand purchases of off-farm products every year simply can't adequately feed people—or profit farmers or protect water and soil quality—in more and more areas of the world.

No one knows what's really possible if trade, development and research were concentrated on meeting each nation's food needs through organic agriculture.

Discounted until recently as a viable approach to food sufficiency, regenerative organic systems are infinitely adaptable across the globe. They combine local wisdom, cultural strengths and advanced biological techniques to carefully utilize local and on-farm resources. These systems are uniquely able to withstand the pressure of diminishing fossil fuel supplies, costly synthetic inputs and patent-controlled genetics while actually fighting climate change through increasing soil organic matter over time.

Start with the Basics

The fact is, no one knows what's really possible if trade, development and research were concentrated on meeting each nation's food needs through organic agriculture grown as locally as is practical. Maybe Colin Tudge is right when he says "Feeding people is easy." In an essay on his book of the same name, the English science writer says the world's communities could easily feed themselves, well, if feeding people were the well-crafted focus of international land-use and agricultural management—rather than an incidental aspect of the industrial food system.

Key points, he says, would be to:

- Raise staple crops (cereals, pulses, nuts and tubers) for basic energy and protein. Use prime farmland for high-value horticultural crops of fruit and vegetables.

- Fit in livestock where cows can have grass in meadows and where hogs and chickens can be fed largely on surpluses and leftovers.

- And basically fit mixed-enterprise farming to the land and climate with an eye for optimizing food value in sustainable ways.

"In general," Tudge says, "Farms should be mixed and must therefore be labour intensive—because well-balanced farms are complex and need very high standards of husbandry."

He says farming that we need is Enlightened Agriculture, based on sound biology and common sense. Raising food in this way, making the best of land for producing the nutrients that humans need most would have us eating "plenty of plants, not much meat, and maximum variety," Tudge says in an essay from May, 2007.

Well, if not easy, then at least easier when the food economy is re-oriented to do two things:

1. Better accommodate the need for healthy subsistence for everyone (increasing demand for fresh, seasonal, nutrient-dense and diverse crops).

2. Bring the true cost of input-intensive and ecologically risky foods to the marketplace (bringing some pricing equity to meat produced humanely on pasture v. in factory-farmed confinement settings).

"How ironic that we must ask our policymakers to make the nutritional health and well-being of their people a nation's first agricultural priority," said Mark Winne, author of "Closing the Food Gap," when asked this week about the fastest way to get a "sustainable food first" shift going in the United States.

Policy changes backed by new commitments to meet basic food needs in sustainable ways can have a huge impact on land use wherever food is grown in food-insecure areas. "Preservation of the biodiversity and other natural resources is a prerequisite for the long-term food security and the eradication of poverty in developing countries," said Amadou Makhtar Diop, international director at the Rodale Institute, reflecting on his many years of work with African agricultural development.

Former U.S. President Bill Clinton said today's global food crisis shows "we all blew it . . ." by treating food crops as commodities instead of as a vital right of the world's poor.

Especially from work in his native Senegal, Diop is convinced that, "Integrated crop-livestock systems reduce risk, contribute to the sustainability of smallholder farmers, improve diet through addition of protein, increase income opportunities and contribute to the restoration of soil organic matter."

Clinton: Food Not a Commodity

Speaking in October [2008] on World Food Day, former U.S. President Bill Clinton said today's global food crisis shows "we all blew it, including me when I was president," by treating food crops as commodities instead of as a vital right of the world's poor. He said that over the long term, only agricultural self-sufficiency could take a significant bite out of world hunger and stave off future financial woes.

"We should go back to a policy of maximum agricultural self-sufficiency," Clinton said. While there would always be a global market for crops like rice, wheat and corn, he added, "it is crazy for us to think we can develop a lot of these countries where I work without increasing their capacity to feed themselves and treating food like it was a color television set."

His recommendations were hardly radical, except in their embrace of common sense. He called for an increase in fair-trade provisions, direct-marketing arrangements and other policies designed to level the playing field between agricultural producers in developed countries and the mostly small farmers who are responsible for the lion's share of worldwide food production.

That's the "what" side of the equation, the "quit stacking the deck against food security" part. The "how" part looks something like this, as outlined recently by Katharine Koon:

- Encourage biodiversity, intensive management and the skilful integration of crop and livestock enterprises that can bring cascading levels of benefits to families with even a small amount of land. Consider these benefits to the 750 million people subsisting on less than $1 a day living in rural areas of the rural global South. This population depends on smallholder farming, selling labor, or a combination of the two.

- By developing these household farms close to home, the farmer—usually a woman—can more easily manage her childcare and cooking duties. This improves childhood nutrition, proper development of children and the likelihood that children—particularly girls—will stay in school.

- By focusing first on optimizing the nutritional value of food crops, family health improves.

- Food raised without external inputs decreases the need for the farmer to work for wages (especially low-paid for women) off the farm to pay for basic food and every-season agricultural inputs.

- Polyculture farms provide multiple species of micro-nutrient-rich plant and animal food.

Finding the ways that can help communities to feed themselves includes what happens in the field, but also what those field practices mean beyond the field edge, as well. Regenerative organic systems—built on natural systems that improve soil organic matter and biodiversity—bring improvements for the farming families, their neighbors, their watershed, their overall community health and the amount of entrepreneurial freedom they have to grow their most sustainable crops in volumes that give them enough to sell to their community and beyond.

These soil-based improvements are documented in Rodale Institute research results, which show carbon sequestration (trapping) of up to 2,000 pounds of carbon per acre per year—far better than no-till using conventional fertilizer and weed-killers. Since it began improving its soils more than 30 years ago, staff has never used synthetic fertilizers, herbicides, pesticides or fungicides. Further, the Institute—in accordance with the USDA's [U.S. Department of Agriculture] National Organic Program—uses no Genetically Modified (GM) crops in its organic fields.

GM Crops Not the Answer

Despite a recent flurry of suggestions that 2008's critically low global food reserves demand even greater use of GM crops, these input-dependent and farmer-unfriendly varieties actually lock in an extreme version of conventional farming. Bred to survive herbicides that kill everything else in the field—or perhaps to produce their own version of a bug-killing bacteria throughout the entire growing season—they are a bio-manipulation strategy that marches in the opposite of the biodiversity trends and genetic weed tolerance that organic farmers seek in their system and crop choices. While they increased convenience for farmers, the heavy reliance on the linked herbicides is causing spray-resistant weeds to emerge, requiring more types of spray or the addition of mechanical weed control—defeating a primary alleged benefit.

"There is no evidence that currently available genetically engineered crops strengthen drought tolerance or reduce fertilizer use. Nor do they fundamentally increase yields," the Union of Concerned Scientists concluded in an overview published earlier this year.

Deteriorating soils are a contributing factor to the drop in world food reserves, according to a report issued by the International Assessment of Agricultural Knowledge, Science and Technology (IAASTD) in May 2008. Failure to use soil-conserving practices, decreased rainfall, destruction of cover vegetation and lack of adding soil organic matter has led to more than 20 percent of the world's cropland being considered as degraded, cutting food production by one-sixth, the World Resources Institute reports.

Once the negative outcomes of soil loss are linked non-sustainable production systems, soil-conserving and soil-building farming will become relatively more profitable because it can compete fairly on its human, agricultural and ecological benefits.

Better soil quality managed through adding organic matter is the basis for fighting global hunger, the U.N.-sponsored IAASTD report concluded. The multiple organizations that supported the findings of some 400 researchers looked at the evidence and found that the most sustainable farming was also the most viable way to meeting the world's basic food needs.

"Yield data just by itself makes the case for a focused and persistent move to regenerative organic farming systems," said Dr. Tim LaSalle, CEO of the Rodale Institute, in "The Organic Green Revolution." "When we also consider that organic systems are building the health of the soil, sequestering CO_2, cleaning up the waterways and returning more economic yield to the farmer, the argument for an organic green revolution becomes overwhelming."

Enlightened Agriculture Is the Key to Future Farming and Meat Production

Colin Tudge

Colin Tudge is a British science writer and the author of numerous books on food, agriculture, and genetics, most notably Feeding People Is Easy *and* The Secret Life of Trees.

I am struck, every hour of every day, by the contrast between what could be in this world, and what is. In particular, everyone who is ever liable to be born could be well fed, forever, not simply on basic provender [dry food, typically for livestock] but to the highest standards of nutrition and gastronomy. That is not all that matters of course but if we get the food right then everything else that we need and want in life—good health, fine landscapes, the company of other species, peace, amity, personal fulfillment—can start to fall into place. The title of my new book—*Feeding People Is Easy*—is a slight exaggeration, but only slight. The necessary techniques and wisdom, and the good will, are all out there. So why aren't we doing the things that are so obvious? Why is the world in such a mess and getting worse? And what must we do to put things right?

Enlightened Agriculture

Most obviously, if we, humanity, seriously want to feed ourselves well, then we need to farm expressly for that purpose—create what I portentously call "Enlightened Agriculture". The bedrock is sound biology and common sense. Focus first on the staple crops—cereals, pulses, nuts, tubers—that provide the bulk of our energy and protein. Devote the best land to

Colin Tudge, "Feeding People Is Easy," Colintudge.com, May 2007. Reproduced by permission.

horticulture—fruit and vegetables. But then—for we don't need to be vegan, and crops grow better if there are animals around—fit in the livestock as and when. Cattle and sheep should graze and—especially in the tropics—browse on the leaves of trees, up on the hills and in the damp meadows and woods where cereal is hard to grow, and pigs and poultry should be fed as they always used to be on surpluses and leftovers. In general, farms should be mixed and must therefore be labour intensive—because well-balanced farms are complex and need very high standards of husbandry.

Now comes a series of wondrous serendipities. Farms that are rooted in common sense and sound biology produce plenty of plants, not much meat, and maximum variety. And here in nine words—plenty of plants, not much meat, and maximum variety—is a summary of all the worthwhile nutritional advice that has flowed in a million articles and bestsellers and TV programmes from all the world's most learned committees this past 30 years. Yet there is more. For here too is the basic structure of all the world's great traditional cuisines—Provence, Tuscany, Turkey, North Africa, China, India. All their finest recipes are variations on this simple theme: lots of plants, not much meat, and maximum variety.

The food chain we have now is not designed to feed people. . . . It is designed to produce the maximum amount of cash in the shortest time.

In other words, the produce from farms that are designed along lines of sound biology to supply the maximum amount of food, kindly and sustainably, also accords precisely with the recommendations of the world's leading nutritionists and—most wondrously of all—with all the world's greatest cuisine. To feed ourselves well we don't even have to be austere. We simply have to indulge in the world's greatest cooking. The future belongs not to the ascetic, but to the gourmet.

Cash-Based Farming

But the food chain we have now is not designed to feed people. In line with the modern cure-all—the allegedly free global market—it is designed to produce the maximum amount of cash in the shortest time. Stated thus, our approach to our most important material endeavour seems unbelievably crass—but that is how things are nonetheless.

The global free market might be good for some things (perhaps we get better computers and warships that way) but for farming, and hence for humanity as a whole, it is disastrous. The simplistic business rules that may (or may not) apply to other enterprises are fatal to Enlightened Agriculture and so, since we depend on agriculture absolutely, they are proving fatal for us.

When cash rules, sound biology goes to the wall and common sense and humanity are for wimps. The goal must be to maximize whatever is most expensive—which means livestock. So now we feed well over half the staples that could be feeding us, to cattle, pigs, and poultry. So instead of helping us to feed ourselves, our animals compete with us. By 2050, on present trends, the world's livestock will consume enough to feed four billion people—equal to the total population of the early 1970s, when the United Nations held its first international conference to discuss the world's food crisis. That livestock will mostly be consumed by people already weighed down with too much saturated fat—for the moment mostly in the west, but increasingly in India and China. The poor will remain poor. So will most farmers. The traders and their shareholders will grow rich. For this, forests are felled and the last of the world's fresh water is squandered—for example on the soya of Brazil, grown to feed the cattle of Europe and now their biggest agricultural earner.

Cash-based farming is not mixed, because that is complicated and labour must be cut and cut again to save costs. So we have cereals from horizon to horizon, cocooned in pesticide, while piggeries in the United States (and soon in Europe, with American backing and European taxpayers' cash) sometimes harbour a million beasts apiece—unbelievably foul and each producing in passing as much ordure as Manchester. Such farming is dangerous. To save money, corners must be cut. Britain's epidemics of foot and mouth disease and BSE [bovine spongiform encephalopathy, or Mad Cow Disease] were not acts of God. They were brought about by cut-price husbandry. The same government that lectures us on health and safety came close, with BSE, to killing us all off.

Worst of all, though—at least in the immediate term—cut-price monocultural farming puts people out of work. That is what it is designed to do. Countries with the fewest farmers are deemed to be the most "advanced". Britain and the US are the world's brand leaders, with about one per cent of their workforce full time on the land. Both eke out their rural workforce with immigrant labour of conveniently dubious legal status who can be seriously underpaid—but we don't talk about that, and in any case that's the market, and the market must rule. In the US, there are more people in jail than full-time on the land. In both countries, prisons are a major growth industry.

In the Third World, 60 per cent of people live on the land. If poor countries industrialize their farming as Britain and the US have done, and as they are increasingly pressured to do, then this would put two billion out of work. Unemployment is the royal road to destitution: what a dreadful joke the "war on poverty" really is. Alternative industries are promised, but there are none on the horizon and cannot be—for no "alternative" can employ the numbers that farming does. There aren't enough resources for all the world to be as industrial as Britain is. Now, one billion people are living in urban slums. There seems to be a vague feeling in high places that this is a temporary state of affairs—but in truth, slums too are a growth industry, or would be if their inhabitants could pay taxes.

In reality, then, our food problems are of two kinds. The first is to grow food well, get it to people, and then cook it properly. That should be fairly straightforward. Far, far harder is to circumvent the corporates and their attendant governments. New Labour has applied the same general strategy to food as to all things: to sell off the assets to the highest bidders and to hand the reins and profits to the corporates, which in this case means Tesco, Monsanto, and the makers of agrochemicals. The aim is not to grow good food, but to maximize cash. That, in all ways, is immensely destructive. In short, the greatest threat to humanity comes from our own leaders. Now that really is a problem.

A Solution

Solution cannot be found through patient reform—for the powers-that-be cannot change to the extent that is needed without sawing off the branch they sit on. Direct confrontation—all out revolution—is pointless because the world's leading governments grant themselves new powers with each passing week.

But there is a third option: Renaissance. People who actually give a damn must just start doing the things that obviously need doing, and ignore the powers-that-be: let Tesco and the rest whither on the vine. Gandhi would surely have approved. In my new book I float the idea of "The Worldwide Food Club": a cooperative of farmers and preparers (cooks, brewers, bakers, charcutiers [butchers]) on the one hand, who want above all to provide good food by the best possible means; and of consumers on the other, who are happy to pay a proper price for food properly produced. To be sure, the movement must begin with the relatively affluent. But cheap food is not really cheap and in any case we should ask why countries like Britain and the US which claim to have such successful economies should have so many poor people. Certainly the answer to poverty does not lie with an economy that is designed to make the rich richer.

The Club must work because it is what most people want—or if not most, then at least a critical mass. Only a monster could be satisfied with the world as it is. Only the most hopeless optimist could suppose that with present strategies, things can get better. Most of what is needed is already out there—The Soil Association and the growing ranks of organic farmers, and other farmers dedicated to "kind" food; excellent bakers and cooks who know exactly what is needed, and care; fair trade movements; the Slow Food Movement, which emphasises the unbreakable link between sound farming and great cooking; that minority of scientists and technologists who are not employed simply to strengthen the corporate hand but ARE truly TUNED to the needs of humanity. It is just a question of bringing it all together into one coherent cause. That cause, in one phrase, I suggest is "Enlightened Agriculture"—and that, the bit that really counts, really should be easy.

Organizations to Contact

The editors have compiled the following list of organizations concerned with the issues debated in this book. The descriptions are derived from materials provided by the organizations. All have publications or information available for interested readers. The list was compiled on the date of publication of the present volume; the information provided here may change. Be aware that many organizations take several weeks or longer to respond to inquiries, so allow as much time as possible.

American Meat Institute (AMI)
1150 Connecticut Ave. NW, 12th Floor
Washington, DC   20036
(202) 587-4200 • fax: (202) 587-4300
Web site: www.meatami.com

The American Meat Institute (AMI) is a national trade association that represents companies that process 95 percent of red meat and 70 percent of turkey in the United States and their suppliers throughout America. AMI monitors legislation, regulation, and media activity that impacts the meat and poultry industry and it provides updates and analyses to its members to help them stay informed. The group's Web site provides links, articles, testimony, and news information from an industry point of view about issues such as animal welfare, the environment, and food safety.

Animal Agriculture Alliance
PO Box 9522, Arlington, Virginia   22209
(703) 562-5160
e-mail: info@animalagalliance.org
Web site: www.animalagalliance.org

The Animal Agriculture Alliance promotes the role of animal agriculture in providing a safe, abundant food supply for the world. The organization seeks to educate consumers, teachers, and the media, serves as a resource for information about animal production, monitors emerging issues, and promotes the development of animal care guidelines. The group's Web site is a source of articles and information about the various issues surrounding factory farming from an industry point of view. Examples of articles include "Animal Rights Extremists Pose an Escalating Risk to Animal Agriculture," "Antibiotics in Livestock Help Humans," and "Agriculture's Commitment to Animal Well-Being."

Center for Food Safety (CFS)

660 Pennsylvania Ave. SE, Suite 302, Washington, DC   20003
(202) 547-9359 • fax: (202) 547-9429
Web site: www.centerforfoodsafety.org

The Center for Food Safety (CFS) is a nonprofit public interest and environmental advocacy membership organization established in 1997 for the purposes of challenging harmful food production technologies and promoting sustainable alternatives. CFS's activities include litigation, advocacy on various sustainable agriculture and food safety issues, as well as public education, grassroots organizing, and media outreach. The organization's Web site contains information about a variety of food-related issues. One example is "What's Wrong with Factory Farming," a compilation of statistics about factory farming.

Center for Science in the Public Interest

1875 Connecticut Ave. NW, Suite 300, Washington, DC   20009
(202) 332-9110 • fax: (202) 265-4954
Web site: www.cspinet.org

The Center for Science in the Public Interest is an advocate for nutrition and health, food safety, alcohol policy, and sound science. The organization produces a newsletter, *Nutrition Action Healthletter*, and its Web site provides numerous articles and reports on the issue of factory farming.

Farm Forward

PO Box 4120, Portland, OR 97208-4120
(877) 313-3276 • fax: (319) 856-1574
Web site: www.farmforward.com

Incorporated in 2007, Farm Forward is a nonprofit advocacy group that seeks to transform the way the United States eats and farms from the present factory farming model to humane and sustainable farming methods. The group's Web site offers basic information about factory farming, including sections on victories in the fight for sustainable farming.

Farm Santuary

3100 Aikens Road (use PO Box 150 for mail service)
Watkins Glen, NY 14891
(607) 583-2225, ext. 233
Web site: http://farmsanctuary.org

Farm Sanctuary was incorporated in 1986 as an advocacy organization for farm animals. Since then, the group has conducted numerous investigative campaigns to uncover cruelty at factory farms, stockyards, and slaughterhouses; campaigned to prevent animal cruelty; and worked to encourage legal and policy reforms that promote respect and compassion for farm animals. The organization also runs the largest rescue and refuge network for farm animals in North America. The Farm Sanctuary Web site contains information about the negative effects of factory farming and about legislative efforts to address these problems.

**The Humane Society of the United States (HSUS),
Factory Farming Campaign**

2100 L St. NW, Washington, DC 20037
(202) 452-1100
Web site: http://www.hsus.org/farm/about/hsus_and_farm_animal_advocacy.html

The Humane Society of the United States is the largest animal protection organization in the nation. Through its Factory Farming Campaign, it strives to take a leadership role on farm animal advocacy issues through legal means, lobbying, research, abuse investigations, and community support. The Web site of the Factory Farming Campaign provides information about factory farming, including various reports and brochures, news articles, and updates on litigation and legislation in this area. Examples of HSUS publications include "Help Farm Animals . . . Follow the Three Rs," "Farm Animal Slaughter and Consumption Statistics," and "A Brief Guide to Egg Carton Labels and Their Relevance to Animal Welfare."

Pew Commission on Industrial Farm Animal Production (PCIFAP)

c/o The John Hopkins Bloomberg School of Public Health
615 N. Wolfe Street, Baltimore, MD   21205
Web site: www.ncifap.org

The independent Pew Commission on Industrial Farm Animal Production (PCIFAP) was formed to conduct a comprehensive, fact-based, and balanced examination of key aspects of the farm animal industry. On April 29, 2008, the commission issued a comprehensive report of its findings, *Putting Meat on the Table: Industrial Farm Animal Production in America*. The report is available on the PCIFAP Web site, as well as a variety of other reports, articles, and testimony on issues relating to factory farming.

Union of Concerned Scientists (UCS)

Two Brattle Square, Cambridge, MA   02238-9105
(617) 547-5552 • fax: (617) 864-9405
Web site: www.ucsusa.org

The Union of Concerned Scientists (UCS) is a science-based nonprofit organization that works for a healthy environment and a safer world. UCS combines independent scientific research and citizen action to develop solutions to environmental and health problems and to secure responsible changes in government policy, corporate practices, and consumer choices. The UCS Web site is a good source of information about industrial agriculture and factory farming. UCS publications on this topic include, for example, "Hidden Costs of Industrial Agriculture," "Industrial Agriculture: Features and Policy," and "Prescription for Trouble: Using Antibiotics to Fatten Livestock."

World Society for the Protection of Animals (WSPA)
89 Albert Embankment, London   SE1 7TP
   England
+44 (0)20 7587 5000 • fax: +44 (0)20 7793 0208
e-mail: wspa@wspa-international.org
Web site: www.wspa-international.org

The World Society for the Protection of Animals (WSPA) is the world's largest alliance of animal welfare societies, with a network of more than 900 member organizations in over 150 countries. The group promotes animal welfare in four key areas—companion animals, farm animals, commercial exploitation of wildlife, and caring for animals affected by natural disasters. In the area of factory farming, WSPA sets up model farms to demonstrate how farmers can improve animal welfare, and the WSPA Web site contains articles about this work and other factory farming issues, as well as providing news about animal welfare issues.

Bibliography

Books

Harvey Blatt   *America's Food: What You Don't Know About What You Eat*, Cambridge, MA: The MIT Press, 2008.

Susan Bourette   *Meat: A Love Story*, New York: Putnam, 2008.

Terence J. Centner *Empty Pastures: Confined Animals and the Transformation of the Rural Landscape*, Champaign, IL: University of Illinois Press, 2004.

Paul K. Conkin   *Revolution Down on the Farm: The Transformation of American Agriculture Since 1929*, Lexington, KY: University Press of Kentucky, 2008.

Michael Conn   *The Animal Research War*, New York: and James Parker Palgrave Macmillan, 2008.

Marian Stamp   *The Future of Animal Farming:*
Dawkins, Roland   *Renewing the Ancient Contract*,
Bonney, and Peter Hoboken, NJ: Wiley-Blackwell, 2008.
Singer

Gail A. Eisnitz   *Slaughterhouse: The Shocking Story of Greed, Neglect, and Inhumane Treatment Inside the U.S. Meat Industry*, Amherst, NY: Prometheus Books, 2006.

Farm Sanctuary and Mary Tyler Moore — *Life Behind Bars: The Sad Truth About Factory Farming*, Watkins Glen, NY: Farm Sanctuary Production, 2004.

Roger Horowitz — *Putting Meat on the American Table: Taste, Technology, Transformation*, Baltimore, MD: The Johns Hopkins University Press, 2005.

John E. Ikerd — *Crisis and Opportunity: Sustainability in American Agriculture*, Lincoln, NE: Bison Books, 2008.

Andrew Kimbrell, ed. — *Fatal Harvest: The Tragedy Of Industrial Agriculture*, Sausalito, CA: Foundation for Deep Ecology, 2002.

Erik Marcus — *Meat Market: Animals, Ethics, and Money*, Cupertino, CA: Brio Press, 2005.

Adrian Morrison — *An Odyssey with Animals: A Veterinarian's Reflections on the Animal Rights & Welfare Debate*, New York: Oxford University Press, 2009.

Willie Nelson — *Farm Aid: A Song for America*, Emmaus, PA: Rodale Books, 2005.

Danielle Nierenberg — *Happier Meals: Rethinking the Global Meat Industry*, Washington, DC: Worldwatch Institute, 2005.

Nicolette Hahn Niman — *Righteous Porkchop: Finding a Life and Good Food Beyond Factory Farms*, New York: William Morrow, 2009.

Michael Pollan   *The Omnivore's Dilemma: A Natural History of Four Meals*, Boston: Penguin, 2007.

Paul Roberts   *The End of Food*, Boston: Mariner Books, 2009.

Matthew Scully   *Dominion: The Power of Man, the Suffering of Animals, and the Call to Mercy*, New York: St. Martin's Griffin, 2003.

Periodicals

Mike Adams   "Factory Animal Farms Produce Meat Through Routine Torture and Environmental Destruction," *Natural News*, October 8, 2007. www.naturalnews.com/022101.html.

Angela Balakrishnan   "Key Findings of Food Crisis Report," *Guardian*, April 15, 2008. www.guardian.co.uk.

Catherine Brahic   "Cows, Pigs and Sheep: Environment's Greatest Threats?" *New Scientist*, December 12, 2006.

Michelle Chen   "Giant Factory Farms Encroach on Communities, Evade Regulation," *Standard News*, July 3, 2006. http://newstandardnews.net.

Karen DeQuasie   "The Myth of Factory Farms," *Manure Matters*, Summer 2003.

Johanne Dion "The Factory Farm and Air Pollution," *On Earth*, February 20, 2009. www.onearth.org.

Collin Dunn "Is a Big Hunk of Steak Worth Almost 2,000 Gallons of Water?" *The Huffington Post*, June 26, 2008. www.huffingtonpost.com.

Sheila Franklin "Factory Farming vs. Sustainable Farming," *Associated Content*, June 12, 2006. www.associatedcontent.com.

C. Holdredge "Blame Factory Farming, Not Organic Food," *Nature*, 2007. www.nature.com.

Brandon Keim "Swine Flu Ancestor Born on U.S. Factory Farms," *Wired Science*, May 1, 2009. www.wired.com.

Mia MacDonald "China Encounters Factory Farming," *China Dialogue*, July 9, 2009. www.chinadialogue.net.

Bill McKibben "A Carnivore Nation's Dilemma," *Trust Magazine*, October 1, 2008. www.pewtrusts.org.

Marlys Miller "Death on a Factory Farm," *Pork Magazine*, March 3, 2009. www.porkmag.com.

New York Times "A Factory Farm Near You," July 31, 2007.

New York Times "The Worst Way of Farming," May 31, 2008.

Danielle Nierenberg	"Factory Farming in the Developing World: In Some Critical Respects, This Is Not Progress at All," *World Watch*, May 1, 2003.
Michael Pollan	"Farmer in Chief," *New York Times*, October 12, 2008.
Matt Ransford	"Factory Farming and Its Dire Consequences," *Popular Science*, March 25, 2008.
Science Daily	"Routine Feeding of Antibiotics to Livestock May Be Contaminating the Environment," July 13, 2007.
Jeff Tietz	"Boss Hog," *Rolling Stone*, December 14, 2006.
Tanya Tolchi	"Wasting Away: Big Agribusiness Factory Farms Make a Big Mess," *Multinational Monitor*, July 28, 2005.
Kerry Trueman	"You Heard It on Oprah: Factory Farms Stink," *The Huffington Post*, October 15, 2008. www.huffingtonpost.com.
Rick Weiss	"Report Targets Costs of Factory Farming," *The Washington Post*, April 30, 2008, p. A02.

Index